HELPING YOUR CHILD WITH

Maps&Globes

GoodYearBooks

are available for most basic curriculum subjects plus many enrichment areas. For more GoodYearBooks, contact your local bookseller or educational dealer. For a complete catalog with information about other GoodYearBooks, please write:

GoodYearBooks
Scott Foresman
1900 East Lake Avenue
Glenview, IL 60025

Cover illustration by Stephen Mach
Design by Christine Ronan

ISBN 0-673-36131-4

5 6 7 8 9-MH-02 01 00 99 98 97

HELPING YOUR CHILD WITH
Maps&Globes

Bruce Frazee   **William Guardia**

GoodYearBooks

An Imprint of ScottForesman
A Division of HarperCollinsPublishers

Acknowledgements

We appreciate Trinity University and the San Antonio Independent School District, especially Ira Ogden Elementary School, for providing support and children to field test lessons.

We are eternally grateful to Ms. Debbie Alaniz for her patience, input, and preparation of the manuscript. Debbie's contribution to the production of the text was valuable not only for her word processing skills, but her keen ability to critique and consult with us from a classroom teacher's perspective.

To our family and friends who tolerated the time spent away from them, especially Bruce William Frazee (5 years old) and Felicia Frazee (9 years old), who also enjoyed learning about maps and globes as we wrote and taught these lessons.

Most of all we hope to help the children who will need to learn how to read maps in a fast-paced, ever-changing, global world.

Best wishes as you enter and enjoy the fascination of maps.

Bruce Frazee
William Guardia

Table of Contents

From *Helping Your Child with Maps & Globes* published by Good Year Books. Copyright © 1994 by Bruce Frazee and William Guardia.

Level 1:

Chapter 2, Level 2:

From *Helping Your Child with Maps & Globes* published by Good Year Books. Copyright © 1994 by Bruce Frazee and William Guardia.

From *Helping Your Child with Maps & Globes* published by Good Year Books. Copyright © 1994 by Bruce Frazee and William Guardia.

Chapter 4, Level 2:

From *Helping Your Child with Maps & Globes* published by Good Year Books. Copyright © 1994 by Bruce Frazee and William Guardia.

From *Helping Your Child with Maps & Globes* published by Good Year Books. Copyright © 1994 by Bruce Frazee and William Guardia.

From *Helping Your Child with Maps & Globes* published by Good Year Books. Copyright © 1994 by Bruce Frazee and William Guardia.

Introduction

Learning to read maps and globes is an important everyday problem-solving skill. Travel, news reports, weather reports, current events, and many occupations all require the ability to read and understand maps. Countless maps appear on television, newspapers, and textbooks, as well as at train, bus, or subway stops. Early exposure to and experiences with maps will help children develop the basic skills needed for using maps both in school and in life.

Maps contain useful information which only becomes understandable to children after they have been taught how to make, read, and use maps. When started early, children begin to understand and appreciate the many uses of maps as they seek answers to past, present, and future events. As we move towards an informational and global society, it is crucial that parents and teachers help young children develop map reading skills.

Sadly, children in our culture seldom study maps nowadays. As adults, we probably remember imagining about distant and exotic places that we wanted to know more about. Today, perhaps because of television, children seem less inquisitive and imaginative when it comes to the study of maps. Studies on Americans' ability to locate peoples and places on maps report low test scores in these areas; in fact, one in five Americans (18–24 years of age) cannot locate the United States on an outline map. This book provides parents and teachers with activities and experiences that will increase children's understanding and skills in map reading.

Preparing to Help Children Learn About Map Reading

Children are naturally curious about and interested in maps. One of the best ways to prepare children for map study is to show a personal interest. Parents and teachers who value the skills involved in map reading and attach importance to map reading in the home and school will help children appreciate and understand maps. Where there are maps, atlases, and globes and discussions at any age level, there is an increased likelihood that children will take an interest and want to know more about people, places, and things that are represented by maps.

Parents and teachers must understand that children learn and develop with different abilities. Experts who study children's growth and development agree that young children who are accustomed to playing and exploring their world become more skillful in learning than those who are deprived of play and exploration situations. This philosophy is important to parents and teachers because playfulness and exploration are important components in developing the beginning skills necessary for young children to understand maps and globes.

Young children tend to view their world in a very self-centered way. They explore their environment or space where they move, but do not consider the relationships between the objects and how those objects relate to themselves. It is important, therefore, for teachers and parents to remember that map reading activities should involve children through the use of their senses and movement. Because children's concept of space is developed from their active movement, sensory experiences, and the surrounding environment, parents and teachers must build upon what children know and then gradually move towards the unknown. Parents are the child's first teachers and can do much to help their child understand maps. Basic map reading readiness begins in the environment where the child lives and plays.

We encourage both parents and teachers to enjoy this text through the games, songs, and activities. This book is easy to use and consists of a wide variety of lessons that engage children in meaningful vocabulary, maps, globes, poetry, songs, writing, and drawing. This active approach helps children to use their senses and make map reading fun.

The following are both general and specific experiences that parents and teachers can provide in order to enrich the child's learning and understanding of maps. These basic suggestions are helpful for children of all ages:

1. Children learn by doing.

2. Provide materials and activities that children can manipulate.

3. Provide children with many maps, globes, and atlases to look at and study.

4. Refer to maps and globes whenever children discuss people, places, or things.

5. Use simple maps and avoid cluttered maps.

6. Show and stress the importance of a map key.

7. Help children discover and see patterns when looking at maps.

8. Spend time talking about maps, showing children maps and answering questions they may have about the information shown on maps.

9. Compare and contrast maps with a globe.

From *Helping Your Child with Maps & Globes* published by Good Year Books. Copyright © 1994 by Bruce Frazee and William Guardia.

10. Use role-playing to show how community helpers rely on maps.

11. Constantly use maps to demonstrate how useful they are in obtaining information.

12. Use many geographical terms and explain their meanings when talking to children.

13. Locate and use many pictures from books and magazines to help associate words with visual images, such as deserts, lakes, rivers, and other natural features.

14. Mark the cardinal directions on a wall in your home or classroom. Use these directions when traveling in and out of your home.

15. Use city or town maps when traveling around the city to point out where children live, as well as friends, relatives, and special places children enjoy visiting.

16. Before taking a field trip or family trip, show children a map of where they will be going, talk about the route, and use the map to show where you are going and how you plan to get there.

17. Keep maps, globes, and atlases easily accessible. Whenever events occur on television or in children's textbooks, encourage them to locate those events on a map.

18. Encourage children to make their own maps using map keys and symbols.

19. Constantly discuss and encourage children's interests in people, places, and things.

20. Allow plenty of time to explore, examine, experiment, and discuss maps.

How to use this book

This book is for parents and teachers to help children learn basic map reading skills. Worksheets accompany each lesson to provide practice, review, and evaluation through a variety of activities. These lessons are designed to help parents and teachers create an environment of curiosity and fun by actively involving the children in each lesson.

Each lesson falls under one of the five major categories that are acknowledged by many professional organizations, including the National Council for Social Studies, which provides information to school districts throughout the nation. These five areas are:

1. Location
2. Direction
3. Scale and Distance
4. Symbols
5. Globe

A definition and explanation is given at the beginning of each category of the major skill areas covered in that section. Specific readiness activities are also suggested to help appraise children's background and previous knowledge about the lessons that will follow in each category.

The lessons in each category are further subdivided into two sections. These sections are divided into Level I lessons, which are simpler, easier, readiness experiences for the younger and beginning child. The Level II lessons begin to develop more complex map reading skills and activities. Generally, children must complete and understand Level I concepts before successfully completing Level II lessons, regardless of age or grade level. Encouragement, discussion, and coverage of the Level I lessons will help to build the readiness necessary to move into the more abstract and complex lessons in Level II lessons. Complete as many of the readiness activities as possible before moving into the lessons.

The Level I activities can be adapted to the needs of Kindergarten or pre-reading children with minimal changes. Read the directions to the children, and if your group is not writing yet, they should be allowed to orally complete the exercises on the worksheets. In any event, give them copies of the worksheets in order to create a print-rich environment and enhance their verbal comprehension.

A question is used as a title for each lesson. This question focuses the map reading skill for parents, teachers, and children. These questions, along with the worksheets, serve as another way to check how much children know about the map reading

4

lesson. Each provides background information, readiness suggestions, or extension activities, depending on the children's familiarity with each question. After the question has been read and discussed, the parent and teacher should spend time focusing, clarifying, and following the rest of the suggestions in each lesson plan. As soon as children have a basic understanding of the skill for a particular lesson, the worksheet can be used as a means to check children's progress.

Because the skill areas are closely interrelated, parents and teachers may want to vary the order in which they approach the activities; if, for example, children are having difficulty with the concept of scale while going through symbol activities, turning to the chapter on Scale and Distance and doing a few of those activities may clear up the confusion. There is no one correct order in which to use this book. Children's needs may dictate a slightly different order than the one outlined in the Table of Contents.

The authors have found these lessons and activities motivational and successful when taught to various groups of children. The more time and creativity parents and teachers provide in developing, encouraging, and teaching the more children's interest will improve their ability to understand and read maps.

Note to Parents

These activities were originally developed for use in the classroom, but many have been adapted for use in the home. Although several lessons refer to the classroom, each lesson can be adapted to the home or neighborhood simply by providing the yard as a playground and the refrigerator or wall as a bulletin board. You may notice that some activities call for an overhead projector; the purpose of the projector is to allow large groups of children see an illustration. If you are working with your child at home, this will not be necessary. You can simply give your child the worksheet that corresponds to the activity.

Chapter One: Symbols

Teaching Children About Symbols

The language of maps is found in the symbols. The map key, or legend, unlocks the meanings of symbols and allows the child to interpret and read maps. Because map symbols are abstract to children, first-hand experiences of the cultural and physical representations of these features should be introduced. Map symbols are representations of real things, so children need to initially devise their own symbols for objects they wish to represent in their immediate environment. Child-made symbols should be used to represent three-dimensional objects (blocks, toy cars, doll houses, furniture), and placed on a map of an area familiar to the children, such as the classroom or playground. When children understand the concept of symbols as representations of real objects through concrete experiences, they can then begin to interpret commercially-prepared map symbols. A map key, the key to interpreting symbols, must accompany each map made by the children. Symbols need to be taught early because they are an important concept used throughout the lessons presented in this and other sections. The ability to interpret symbols is a crucial life-skill ability; the earlier children can experience symbols the sooner they can begin to make sense of their environment and the world.

The following activities will provide children with readiness skills before they begin the lessons that follow for this chapter.

1. Make a three-dimensional map of your home or neighborhood using small milk cartons or boxes to represent buildings. Use buttons and other objects to add variety and symbols to represent other features of your home or neighborhood. Try to keep the scale relationship as accurate as possible.

2. Encourage children to make maps using map keys (legends) with their own choice of symbols.

3. Help children learn colors and locate the various colors on a map. Discuss and describe the use of colors to show the various features on different types of maps.

From *Helping Your Child with Maps & Globes* published by Good Year Books. Copyright © 1994 by Bruce Frazee and William Guardia.

4. Use building blocks to allow children to build maps of an area they know. Let children explain their maps and what the blocks represent.

5. Have children draw their own symbols for their room.

6. Have a boy and a girl stand in the room and have children draw pictures of them. Discuss the real people and the symbols that represent them in the pictures.

7. Show children photographs of different objects: buildings, church, home, streets, school, automobiles, etc. Have them develop and draw symbols for each object.

8. Design a map for a bulletin board in the classroom or refrigerator door at home. Place symbols developed by children in appropriate places.

9. Have children select colors as symbols for different objects to add to the map in #8 above. For example: blue for water, green for grass, brown for mountains, etc.

Skills to be Acquired: Symbols

1. Recognizes symbols look like (represent) real objects.

2. Interprets color as a symbol to represent an object.

3. Interprets and draws his/her own symbols to represent chosen objects.

4. Constructs various landforms which represent real features or landforms.

5. Reads and interprets map symbols.

6. Makes maps showing scale and symbols (rooms, neighborhoods, cities, etc.).

7. Solves problems measuring distances on map.

8. Interprets lines, dots, and colors on maps.

9. Uses legends to find information or make comparisons about an area.

From *Helping Your Child with Maps & Globes* published by Good Year Books. Copyright © 1994 by Bruce Frazee and William Guardia.

10. Draws maps which include keys (legend) titles, direction finder (compass rose) and/or other information.

11. Understands and uses a variety of symbols.

12. Interprets and put geographic data into graphs.

13. Makes graphs to express information and relationships.

14. Reads and makes references from symbols on maps and graphs to obtain information.

15. Locates natural features on maps.

How do You Interpret Symbols?

Concept: To interpret symbols.

Objective: Write a message using a code and a code key.

Materials: Pictures of common symbols and braille books.

Procedure:

1. Explain to the class the importance of symbols and how much we rely on symbols in our world.
2. Show various pictures of common symbols. For example: a traffic light, road signs or numbers.
3. Demonstrate an example of a code so children can interpret the meaning of the symbols.
   For example: X O — # +.

#	=	Good
O	=	Am
—	=	A
X	=	I
+	=	Person

4. Let children write a sentence using a coding system and a key.
5. Let children exchange papers and interpret the codes.

Enrichment/Extension: Show various symbols and discuss their meaning. Obtain braille books and have children feel the pages. Discuss how these symbols are helpful to blind people.

Directions for Worksheet: Help children see relationships between the letters and symbols. Explain that they look at the symbol key to find the correct letter. The letter substitutes for the symbol to make a sentence.

From *Helping Your Child with Maps & Globes* published by Good Year Books. Copyright © 1994 by Bruce Frazee and William Guardia.

How Do You Interpret Symbols?

Directions: Look at the symbols and the key. Interpret the symbols to find the secret message. Use the space below to make your own secret code and message.

Secret message:

___ ___ ___ ___ ___   ___ ___   ___   ___ ___ ___ ___   ___ ___ ___

Secret code (the key):

◆ = A   ✳ = O

▲ = I   ★ = D

✔ = T   ◯ = Y

▢ = S   ◗ = G

My own secret message:

My own secret code key:

Why Do Symbols Represent Real Objects?

From *Helping Your Child with Maps & Globes* published by Good Year Books. Copyright © 1994 by Bruce Frazee and William Guardia.

Level 1

Concept: Symbols represent real objects.

Objective: Interpret and identify common map symbols.

Materials: overhead projector (optional), doll house (scaled-down) objects to represent real objects, and objects to put on overhead.

Procedure:

1. Show children a small car. Ask: "What does this look like?"
2. Place the car sideways on the overhead or trace around the car on a sheet of paper. Attach butcher paper to the chalkboard and trace the outline of the car.
3. Hold up a stop sign. Put the stop sign on the overhead. Trace the outline of the stop sign.
4. Repeat this process with other objects, like model railroad tracks, rice, corn, and money.
5. Explain to children that these shapes represent, or look like, the real objects. These symbols are used as a map key or legend.
6. Locate various map keys and discuss and interpret them.

Enrichment/Extension: Have children create their own map key using various symbols to stand for the real objects.

Directions for Worksheet: Have children study the objects. Give several examples of symbols that could be used to show these objects. Let children make up their own symbols for objects.

Symbols Represent Real Objects

Directions: Look at these objects. Make up a symbol to show each object.

Objects   **Symbols**

1. home:

2. swing:

3. doll:

4. shoe:

5. tree:

6. tall building:

7. car:

8. desk or table:

9. computer:

10. dog:

From *Helping Your Child with Maps & Globes* published by Good Year Books. Copyright © 1994 by Bruce Frazee and William Guardia.

What is a Map Key?

Level 1

Concept: A map key provides information to locate places and understand maps.

Objective: Design a map key for objects in the room.

Materials: Small-scale toys, textbooks, maps, and overhead projector (optional).

Procedure:

1. Discuss big and small objects located in the room. Talk about the impossibility of putting a real object on a map.
2. Discuss the key to a map. Show several maps calling attention to the key. Overhead maps, desk maps, and textbook maps will assist in this lesson.
3. Let the children bring in a picture of themselves and put it on the bulletin board. Ask whether the picture is smaller or larger than they really are.
4. Bring in small cars, dolls, etc. These objects are scaled versions of real objects. Discuss and demostrate these concepts.
5. Let the children think of a way they could scale down the room. Discuss symbols or objects they would use to represent the real objects in the key. Have them create a key that could be used on a map of the room.

Enrichment/Extension: Draw a scale map of the room using some unit of measure, such as hands or a large piece of string. Include the scale and a key on the room map.

Directions for Worksheet: Read the question on the worksheet to the children. Have them mark T for true and F for false.

From *Helping Your Child with Maps & Globes* published by Good Year Books. Copyright © 1994 by Bruce Frazee and William Guardia.

What is a Map Key?

Directions: Look at the map and the map key. Write a T for true and an F for false in front of each sentence.

Map Key

◯ table △ toy

⌂ chair ▯ book

▭ bed ▯ door

〰 window

_____ 1. Sue has books in her room.

_____ 2. Sue has a clock in her room.

_____ 3. There is a table in Sue's room.

_____ 4. Sue has two beds in her room.

_____ 5. There are six toys in Sue's room.

_____ 6. Sue has a window in her room.

From *Helping Your Child with Maps & Globes* published by Good Year Books. Copyright © 1994 by Bruce Frazee and William Guardia.

How are Symbols Used in a Map Key?

Level 1

Concept: A map key contains symbols that stand for a real picture.

Objective: Analyze a picture to create a map key.

Materials: overhead projector (optional) and a transparency of the worksheet.

Procedure:

1. Discuss the fact that a map needs a key to help understand the map.
2. Explain that a map is a smaller picture of a larger area and symbols are used to show objects in that picture.
3. Prepare an overhead transparency from the worksheet and place on the overhead projector. Show top portions first and discuss each of the objects.
4. Show the bottom portion of the transparency, covering the corner with the key. Ask children what each of the objects represents. After discussion, show the key. Stress the importance of looking at a map key whenever you use or draw a map.
5. Give groups of children a simple picture. Have them make a map of the picture.

Enrichment/Extension: Have children visualize a room in their home or school. Have them make a map from this mental image.

Directions for Worksheet: Make a transparency from the worksheet. Show the top portion and discuss the objects on the transparency. Have children locate the objects and their symbols on the bottom portion of the transparency.

From *Helping Your Child with Maps & Globes* published by Good Year Books. Copyright © 1994 by Bruce Frazee and William Guardia.

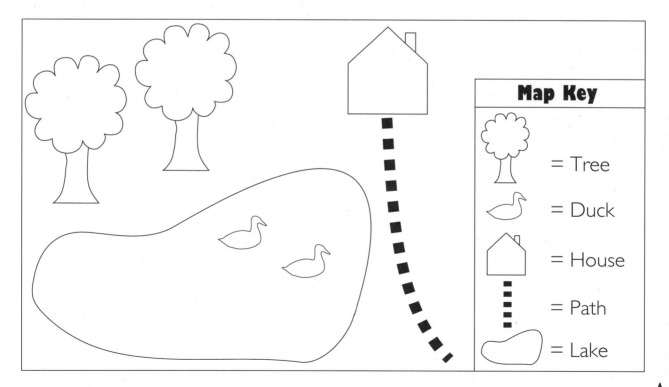

Map Key

= Tree

= Duck

= House

= Path

= Lake

How do you Make a Map Key?

Level 1

Concept: Interpret information from a map key.

Objective: Interpret symbols through the use of a map key.

Materials: Paper, pencils, overhead projector (optional), and several maps with keys.

Procedure:

1. Discuss the fact that each map has a key which provides information for reading the map.
2. Show several maps with keys.
3. Give children five items to symbolize, such as: a person, railroad track, a car, roadways, an animal, hospital, plane, church building, and others that children suggest.
4. Have children draw the symbols on the chalkboard or overhead.
5. Show a picture, let the children make a map using symbols to show the objects in the picture. Make sure children make a key.

Enrichment/Extension: Have children construct a map of the playground or classroom and devise a key with symbols to represent the objects on the map.

Directions for Worksheet: Have children identify and name each object in the picture. Then have children create a symbol for each object in the picture and locate in the proper area on the map below. Have children show the meaning of the symbols in the map key.

From *Helping Your Child with Maps & Globes* published by Good Year Books. Copyright © 1994 by Bruce Frazee and William Guardia.

How do you Make a Map Key?

Directions: Look at the objects in the picture. Name the objects and make a symbol at the bottom right square to represent each object in the picture. Also, make a map key to explain the symbols.

Map Key

From *Helping Your Child with Maps & Globes* published by Good Year Books. Copyright © 1994 by Bruce Frazee and William Guardia.

What Makes Big and Small?

Concept: A map key provides information to interpret symbols.

Objective: Compose a map key for objects in the room.

Materials: Small scaled toys, textbooks, overhead projector (optional).

Procedure:

1. Discuss big and small objects located in the room. Talk about the impossibility of putting a real object on a map.
2. Discuss the map key on a map. Show several maps calling attention to the map keys. Overhead maps, wall maps, and textbooks will assist in this activity.
3. Let children bring in a picture of themselves and put it on the bulletin board. Discuss whether that is really them and if the picture is smaller or larger than they really are.
4. Bring in small cars, dolls, etc. These objects are scaled versions of a real object. Discuss and demonstrate these concepts.
5. Let children think of a way they could scale down the room. Discuss symbols or objects they would use to represent the real objects in the map key. Have them create a map key that could be used on a map of the room.

Enrichment/Extension: Draw a scale map of the room using some unit of measure. Include the scale and the map key on the room map.

Directions for Worksheet: Have children compare symbols that are bigger or smaller than the object they represent. Read the sentences to the children and compare objects as bigger or smaller than the children. Discuss how these objects would look on a map.

From *Helping Your Child with Maps & Globes* published by Good Year Books. Copyright © 1994 by Bruce Frazee and William Guardia.

What Makes Big and Small?

Directions: Circle BIGGER or SMALLER to make the sentence correct.

1. You are a flea.
You are BIGGER or SMALLER than I.

2. You are a school.
You are BIGGER or SMALLER than I.

3. You are a car.
You are BIGGER or SMALLER than I.

4. You are a bee.
You are BIGGER or SMALLER than I.

5. You are a cat.
You are BIGGER or SMALLER than I.

6. You are a book.
You are BIGGER or SMALLER than I.

7. You are a fire fighter.
You are BIGGER or SMALLER than I.

8. You are a boat.
You are BIGGER or SMALLER than I.

9. You are a tree.
You are BIGGER or SMALLER than I.

10. You are a fish.
You are BIGGER or SMALLER than I.

How are Landforms Identified on a Map?

Level 1

Concept: Symbols show landforms on a map.

Objective: Understand that symbols represent various landforms.

Materials: Map of North America and topographic maps.

Procedure:

1. Show a map of North America.
2. Locate various landforms on the map, such as: mountains, rivers, lakes, plains, etc.
3. Have children select colors or symbols to identify the various landforms located.
4. Make a map key using colors or symbols to show the various landforms you identified.
5. Discuss the need for knowing where landforms are located (travel, occupations).

Enrichment/Extension: Give each child a desk top map or a city map. Have each child or groups of children locate various landforms on the map. Discuss how each landform is identified.

Directions for Worksheet: Have the children locate and color the various landforms on the map. Have the children make a color legend to show each landform.

From *Helping Your Child with Maps & Globes* published by Good Year Books. Copyright © 1994 by Bruce Frazee and William Guardia.

Identifying Landforms on a Map

Directions: Look at the map symbols. Color each landform symbol a different color. Color the map to show areas covered by each landform.

Mountains

Hills

Plains

Rivers

Lakes

What are Landforms?

Concept: Recognize various landforms.

Objective: Identify and define various landform shapes.

Materials: Cut-out shapes of various physical features and landforms, maps, textbooks, and an overhead projector (optional).

Procedure:

1. Cut out various shapes to represent islands, peninsulas, capes, archipelagoes. Write the name on the back of the shapes. (See Worksheet)
2. Place a shape on the overhead, or hold it up and ask children to describe what they see.
3. Show children another shape. Discuss the observations.
4. Compare the two shapes to each other. Let children describe the likenesses and differences between the two. List characteristics described by children on the chalkboard.
5. Add another shape. Discuss and compare.
6. Put the shapes on a bulletin board or a special area of the room so children can observe, touch, and compare the various shapes, while having the opportunity to learn the shapes, spelling, and meaning.
7. Pass out world maps or textbook maps and locate the various shapes discussed.

Enrichment/Extension: After children have the opportunity to manipulate and compare the shapes, put them back on the overhead and let children write a statement or description of the shape.

Directions for Worksheet: Have children cut out the squares to use like flashcards. Have them match each square with the correct landform.

From *Helping Your Child with Maps & Globes* published by Good Year Books. Copyright © 1994 by Bruce Frazee and William Guardia.

What are Landforms?

Directions: Choose the name of the landform from the words below and write that word under the correct picture.

Continent   Mountain   River
Island   Plain   Lake

_____   _____   _____

_____   _____   _____

From *Helping Your Child with Maps & Globes* published by Good Year Books. Copyright © 1994 by Bruce Frazee and William Guardia.

How can Products be Shown on a Map?

Level 2

Concept: Symbols are used to show products on a map.

Objective: Understand how symbols show products on a map.

Materials: Product maps and an atlas.

Procedure:

1. Show various product maps.
2. Discuss how these maps help to show where various minerals or crops used by humans can be located by using symbols.
3. Point to the map key. Discuss the symbols and the location of the products using the map key.
4. Discuss certain products people use, such as: iron, diamonds, wheat, oil, aluminum, gold, etc.
5. Ask the class to identify other products people use. Make a map and a map key showing various products the class identified.

Enrichment/Extension: Give each child a product map or a desktop map. Have them choose several products and locate them at various locations on the map. Let children make their own symbols and map keys to show how these products can be identified.

Directions for Worksheet: Have children locate the various products on the map. Have children color the map and map key.

From *Helping Your Child with Maps & Globes* published by Good Year Books. Copyright © 1994 by Bruce Frazee and William Guardia.

Showing Products on a Map

Directions: Look at the map symbols. Color each product symbol a different color. Color the map and the map key to show each product.

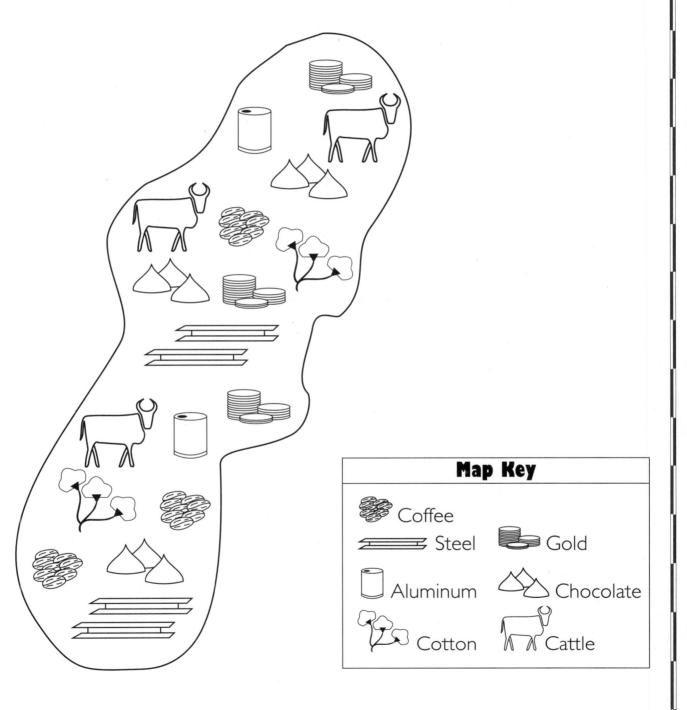

Map Key

- Coffee
- Steel
- Aluminum
- Gold
- Chocolate
- Cotton
- Cattle

How Many People Live in a City?

From *Helping Your Child with Maps & Globes* published by Good Year Books. Copyright © 1994 by Bruce Frazee and William Guardia.

Level 2

Concept: Interpret a map key to find information.

Objective: Use a map key to find the population of a city.

Materials: Crayons and paper.

Procedure:

1. Use the worksheet to determine the population of Alpha State by adding total populations for each city.
2. Say that Alpha State has only ten cities of various sizes. Have children compute the average population for the ten cities.
3. Divide Alpha State into quadrants. Find out the population of the northeast section, southwest, etc.
4. Divide the class into groups of five and assign each group a city and describe the way of life in their city. For example: If the population of "G" was 175,000, what type of people do you think would live in this city? What type of work do people do in this community? What type of homes might you find in this community? Why would you want or not want to live there?

Enrichment/Extension: Let children design a section of the universe with planets of varying size and population. Have them write a paragraph about each planet, telling the name of the people who inhabit the planet, activities of that planet, etc. Have children draw pictures of the different planets and the inhabitants of the planet.

Directions for Worksheet: Discuss the questions and worksheet with the class. Have children fill in the answers as you do the procedures for the lesson.

How Many People Live in a City?

Directions: Look at the map symbols and use the map key to interpret the symbols and answer the questions.

Alpha State

▼ ๐ A

✖ D

◗ C

▲ I

◆ E

■ B

✔ F

● J

★ H

✖ G

Map Key:

▼	=	25,000	✖	=	125,000	● = 200,000
◗	=	50,000	▲	=	150,000	✔ = 225,000
◆	=	75,000	★	=	175,000	✖ = 250,000
■	=	105,000				

Questions:

1. The total population of Alpha State is_____.

2. Draw the symbol that shows the largest city in Alpha State:

3. Draw the symbol that shows the smallest city in Alpha State:

4. Most people live in the _____ part of the state.

5. What is the average population for the cities?_____.

Level 1

Concept: The higher above sea level, the colder the climate.

Objective: Compare altitude with climate.

Materials: Poster board, papier mache, colored markers, and an atlas.

Procedure:

1. Have children construct a cone-like object with poster board or papier mache as illustrated below.
2. Help children locate the various degrees of elevation and separate by using various colors.

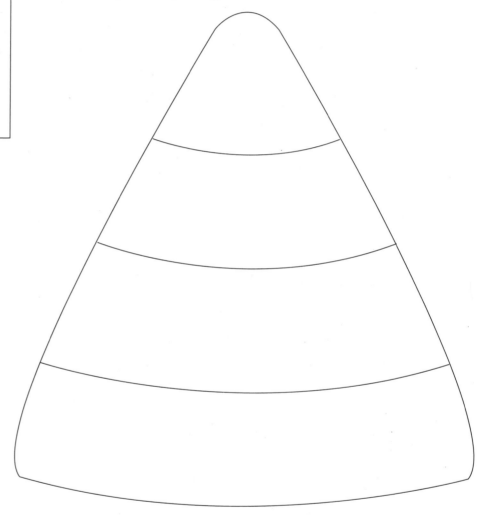

Enrichment/Extension: Ask children to research the climate in various regions and compare to the elevation.

Directions for Worksheet: Assign various colors to degrees of elevation for the cone-like object. With the help of a colored map, locate various altitudes on a United States map.

From *Helping Your Child with Maps & Globes* published by Good Year Books. Copyright © 1994 by Bruce Frazee and William Guardia.

Elevation and Rainfall

Directions: Use various colors to show elevation on the maps below. Make up your own map key to show what each color means.

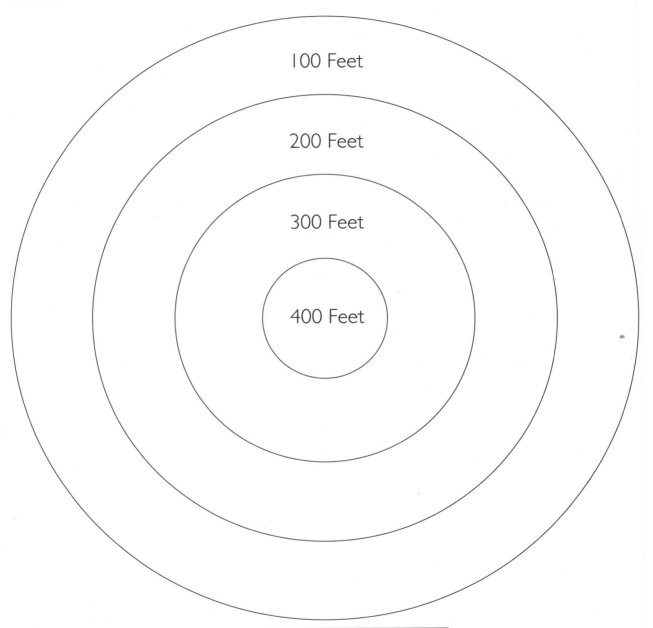

100 Feet

200 Feet

300 Feet

400 Feet

Map Key

	= 100 Feet		= 300 Feet
	= 200 Feet		= 400 Feet

From *Helping Your Child with Maps & Globes* published by Good Year Books. Copyright © 1994 by Bruce Frazee and William Guardia.

Chapter Two: Location

From *Helping Your Child with Maps & Globes* published by Good Year Books. Copyright © 1994 by Bruce Frazee and William Guardia.

Teaching Children About Location

Children must become aware of where they are located in relation to familiar landmarks, such as their homes, schools, or classrooms. Location describes how one place relates to others. Many real-life examples and first-hand experiences should be discussed. Children can initially learn to locate familiar places on maps by manipulating three-dimensional objects that represent things in their immediate environment. Maps made by others are valuable if references are directly and clearly linked to children's experiences. An experience, like a walk around the block or a field trip, gives first-hand meaning to a simple map and provides for comparisons of relative location of objects in relationship to the child's location. Children need to understand that location is relative; in other words, an object on one child's left could be another child's right, depending on the direction they are facing. It is very important and often difficult to get children to understand that they must first discover where they are in order to determine the location of other objects.

The following activities will provide children with readiness skills before they begin the lessons that follow for this chapter.

1. Keep a map and a globe near the television to locate places talked about on various programs.

2. Make sure children know the name of their town and their street address. Help children to describe colors and shape of the home and the location of other features near their home.

3. Show children a map before you take a trip. Discuss where you are going and how you will get there using the map. Discuss the directions and earth's features as you drive.

4. Put together puzzles of the United States or world. Through the placement of the pieces, children use various senses to relate where one place is located in relationship to another.

5. Locate signs in the community. Discuss the need and meaning of these signs in terms of how they can help you locate places.

6. Make a map of a room in the home or school. Have children pretend they are on the ceiling looking down on the room. Have them locate various objects in the room on the map. Encourage accurate scale and symbols for the objects, especially with older children.

7. Have children take a small 6" x 6" square board and place rubber bands up and down and right to left to make a grid. The board will represent the room they are in. Have children locate themselves on the grid according to where they are in the room.

8. Ask children to locate their home and school on a neighborhood map to see the relationship between the location of their home and school. Locate other places near the home, such as the church, park, apartment buildings, rivers, bridges, train tracks, etc.

9. Develop a bulletin board at school, drawing a map of the classroom. Have children locate various objects in the room on the map. Every day, have a surprise object to locate and award a prize for the discovery.

10. Take photographs of different buildings in your city and have children locate the place where the picture was taken. Have children draw other pictures of tall and small buildings to place on the bulletin board map or refrigerator door.

11. Take children to the grocery store. Have them locate various items, such as milk, bread, meat, and fruit. Back home, have children draw a map of the store including the items they located in the appropriate place on the map. Discuss the aisles with reference to longitude or latitude lines.

Skills to be Acquired: Location

1. Locates land and water bodies.

2. Locates self in relation to objects in the environment.

3. Uses terms to describe relative locations.

4. Locates places on a map and a globe.

5. Locates continents.

6. Understands that the shape of the land varies in different locations.

7. Understands that objects are located in a definite direction from each other.

From *Helping Your Child with Maps & Globes* published by Good Year Books. Copyright © 1994 by Bruce Frazee and William Guardia.

8. Locates city, state, country, and continent on a map and a globe.

9. Locates the North and South Poles.

10. Orients location in north, south, east, and west.

11. Locates the equator, tropics, and the hemispheres.

12. Locates places north and south of the equator.

13. Locates places using a grid.

14. Locates objects in the immediate and surrounding environment.

15. Locates the same area on different maps to draw comparisons.

16. Locates the prime meridian and international date line.

17. Gives the direction of other cities, states, continents in terms of cardinal directions.

18. Constructs simple maps to locate places.

19. Locates north at noon.

20. Learns to orient maps to the north.

21. Uses maps to plan trips.

22. Locates rivers, mountains, and other geographical features.

23. Locates areas by interpreting a map legend.

24. Determines latitude and longitude for specific places.

25. Locates natural features.

26. Uses a highway map to plan a trip.

27. Locates areas of distortion on maps and knows why the distortion occurs.

From *Helping Your Child with Maps & Globes* published by Good Year Books. Copyright © 1994 by Bruce Frazee and William Guardia.

Where am I in the World?

Concept: Understand expanded horizons.

Objective: Sequence each component of the expanded environment.

Materials: Eight graduated small to large containers.

Procedure:

1. Obtain nesting blocks, barrel tupperware, or any other container to represent the following concepts:
   a. World
   b. Continent
   c. Country
   d. State
   e. City
   f. Community
   g. Neighborhood
   h. Home
   i. Me

2. Start by using the smallest container as a symbol for "me": to illustrate, say "My name is (fill in your name)." Then pick up the next smallest container, and say, "I live at (home address), pick up next container, "In the (school name) neighborhood," "In the city of (fill in city name)," and so on. Encourage children to do the same. Keep expanding into the largest container, the World. Then, reverse the process.

3. Go through the same expanded environment using various local, state, national, and world maps, and finally the globe.

Enrichment/Extension: Have 9 children wear the following signs: World, Continent, Country, State, City, Community, Neighborhood, Home, and Me. Have children role-play the expanded environment, by aligning themselves in the proper sequence, from largest to smallest, then from smallest to largest.

Directions for Worksheet: To each child, pass out 9 pre-cut circles of paper of the following diameters: 9", 8", 7", 6", 5", 4", 3", 2", and 1". Using an acorn clip, secure the circles in ascending order of size. Discuss that the smallest circle represents Me, next largest Home, etc. Use the worksheet as a model to show the finished product.

From *Helping Your Child with Maps & Globes* published by Good Year Books. Copyright © 1994 by Bruce Frazee and William Guardia.

Where am I in the World?

Directions: Color each circle a different color.

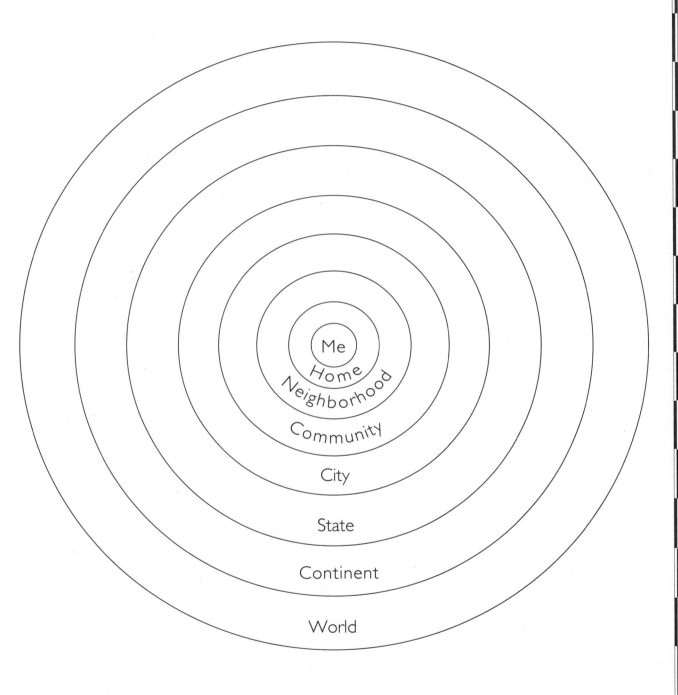

From *Helping Your Child with Maps & Globes* published by Good Year Books. Copyright © 1994 by Bruce Frazee and William Guardia.

Concept: Locate self in relationship to other objects in the classroom.

Objective: Construct a three-dimensional map of the classroom.

Materials: Large appliance box, various three-dimensional objects, and construction paper.

Procedure:

1. Show various types of maps, especially a road map. Also, show the children a globe. Explain that maps represent real places and things.

2. Prepare for this lesson by acquiring a large appliance box and do the following before the lesson:

   a. Cut the box so it has approximately 6-8 inches of cardboard on each side. Note: The sides will represent the walls and the bottom of the box, the floor.

   b. Cut an opening to represent the entrance or door of your classroom. This will also serve as a base for orienting other objects in the classroom. Put the cardinal direction on the proper wall of the box.

   c. Cut colored construction paper to use as symbols for the chalkboard, windows, clock, bulletin board, and any other fixture that is on the classroom walls.

   d. Collect three-dimensional objects such as: matchboxes, blocks, etc. to represent desks, tables, chairs, or other seating arrangements. Write the name of a child on a sheet of paper to represent each class member's seat.

3. Orient the box map to the north wall of the classroom.

4. Select children to locate and attach the various symbol objects to the walls of the classroom box.

5. Select children to locate and attach various symbol objects to the floor of the classroom box.

6. Have children locate and attach their representative seat object to the proper location they occupy.

Enrichment/Extension: Using the classroom box map as a model, have children each draw a map of the classroom on a flat surface. In this activity, children transfer knowledge from the three-dimensional to the two-dimensional.

Directions for Worksheet: Let children complete the worksheet. Have children make their own classroom map and map key following the format used on the worksheet.

From *Helping Your Child with Maps & Globes* published by Good Year Books. Copyright © 1994 by Bruce Frazee and William Guardia.

Directions: Look at the map. Fill in the blanks below.

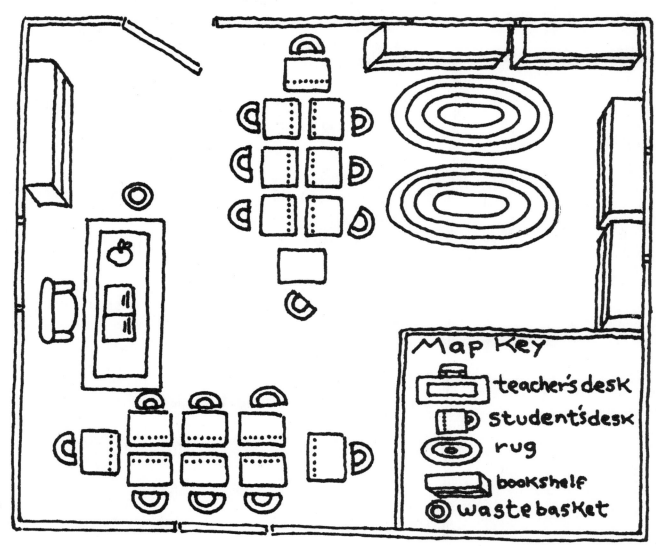

Map Key

teacher's desk
student's desk
rug
bookshelf
wastebasket

1. How many desks are in the classroom? _____

2. The wastebasket is near the _____.

3. Are there rugs in the classroom? _____

4. How many tables are in the classroom?_____

5. Draw the symbol or object to show the bookshelf.

From *Helping Your Child with Maps & Globes* published by Good Year Books. Copyright © 1994 by Bruce Frazee and William Guardia.

Where are the Boys and Girls?

Concept: Locating self in relationship to others.

Objective: Chart the location of boys and girls in the classroom.

Materials: Colored markers and lesson worksheet.

Procedure:

1. Have the children sketch a map of the desk arrangement in the classroom. (See worksheet.)
2. Let the children decide how to symbolically differentiate between the boys' and girls' desks.
   Examples: A. Boys' desks are red, girls' desks are green.
   B. Girls' desks are X's, boys' desks are O's.
3. Make a key to represent children in the classroom and put on each map.
4. Have children write their names in the appropriate desk space.
5. Use the map of desks to let children check daily attendance.

Enrichment/Extension: Have the children make a bar graph to compare the amount of girls and boys in the room. Make a pictograph to represent the total number of boys and girls in the class.

Directions for Worksheet: Have the dhildren sketch a map of the classroom, including the teacher's desk and desks or tables where children sit. Have children write in the names of the children at or near each desk area. Children can use the worksheet to see who is absent and present each day.

From *Helping Your Child with Maps & Globes* published by Good Year Books. Copyright © 1994 by Bruce Frazee and William Guardia.

Where are the Boys and Girls?

Directions: Draw a map of the places where people sit in your classroom, including the teacher. Write your name and the names of other children near the place where they are seated. Mark girls' desks with an X and boys' desks with an O.

Where are you: North, South, East or West?

Concept: Describe location by cardinal directions.

Objective: Describe the location of objects and places by using cardinal directions.

Materials: Cardinal direction signs.

Procedure:

1. Review the cardinal directions. Make sure the walls are properly labeled north, south, east, and west.
2. Discuss the location of specific objects in the room using the cardinal directions. For example: The clock is on the north wall or the chalkboard is on the east wall.
3. Give directions using cardinal terms. For example: Go south to the sink. Go north two steps and west two steps. Use cardinal directions when sending groups or individuals to some school area. For example: Go south to the playground.
4. Go outdoors and play the game "Simon Says." Face east, etc. This will enable children to orient themselves outside the room. Talk about what children see when facing north, south, east, and west.
5. Determine the cardinal direction of various landmarks near your home or school when you come back. Have the children state the directions of the various landmarks in relationship to the room.

Enrichment/Extension: Apply the cardinal directions when locating places mentioned in class discussion on the map and the globe. For example: Determining the direction from one place to another; in school, to restrooms, to the library, etc.; locating places as being north or south of the equator.

Directions for Worksheet: Have children complete the worksheet.

From *Helping Your Child with Maps & Globes* published by Good Year Books. Copyright © 1994 by Bruce Frazee and William Guardia.

North, South, East or West

Directions: Look at the map. Answer the questions by writing the correct direction word in the blank.

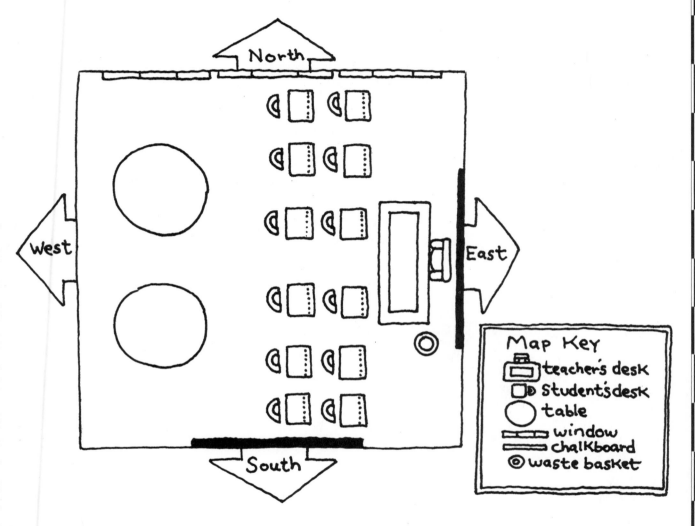

1. The tables are on the _____ side of the room.

2. The chalkboards are on the _____ and _____ walls.

3. The windows are on the _____ side of the room.

4. The teacher's desk is on the _____ side of the room.

5. The wastebasket is on the _____ side of the room.

Which Side of the River?

Concept: Compare location between several objects.

Objective: Determine the number of objects to the north and east of the river.

Materials: Shapes and chalkboard.

Procedure:

1. Draw a vertical line on the chalkboard. Make a key stating that the line represents (looks like) a river.

2. Put several shapes (squares, circles, or triangles) each representing a designated building such as a school house, farm, church, etc. on each side of the river. Note: Make these equal and unequal amounts. Show what each symbol represents in the key.

3. Ask comparative questions such as:
   a. Are there more farms on the east or west side of the river?
   b. Is the church on the east or west side of the river?
   c. Is the school on the east or west side of the river? Draw a horizontal line (river) and repeat the same process but reinforce the directions of north and south.

Enrichment/Extension: Draw horizontal and vertical lines through the center of the classroom. Have children identify the objects in the north, south, east, and west sides of the room.

Directions for Worksheet: Have children complete worksheet.

From *Helping Your Child with Maps & Globes* published by Good Year Books. Copyright © 1994 by Bruce Frazee and William Guardia.

Directions: This is a farm. Find the farm house. Write the direction that each picture is from the farm house.

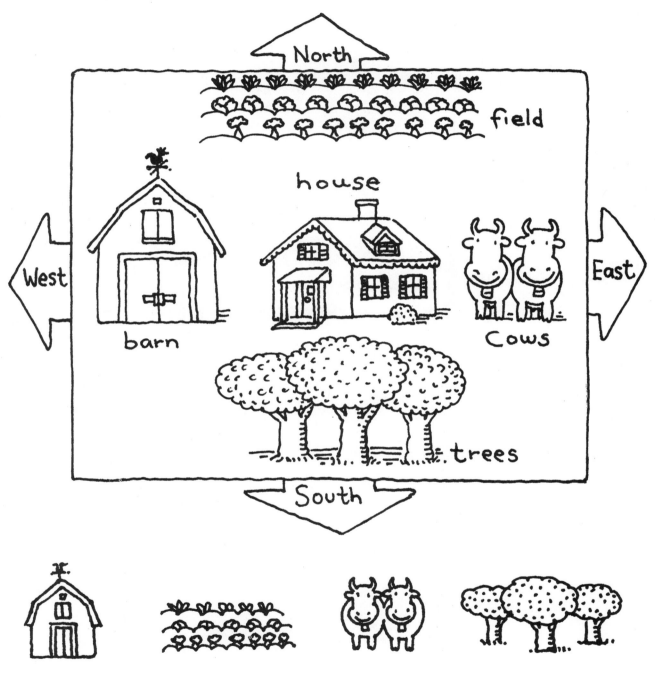

Level 1

Concept: The shape and location of the continents.

Objective: Identify the shape of the continents and place them in the correct positions.

Materials:
Construction paper, overhead projector (optional), wall map, and globe.

Procedure:

1. Place the shape of one continent on the overhead projector or give your child the worksheets. Discuss and describe its characteristics. Repeat this procedure with the other continents.
2. Using a globe, locate the same continent representing the continent. Repeat the procedure with other continents.
3. Using a wall map, locate the continents.

Enrichment/Extension: Put shapes of continents in an activity center. Let the children look at and learn names of the continents. Write several facts about each continent on each shape. Example: Largest country, biggest export, famous landform, etc.

Directions for Worksheet: Have children color and label the seven continents.

1. North America
2. South America
3. Africa
4. Europe
5. Antarctica
6. Australia
7. Asia

From *Helping Your Child with Maps & Globes* published by Good Year Books. Copyright © 1994 by Bruce Frazee and William Guardia.

Where are the Continents?

Directions: Color in the continents and label each continent by its shape.

North America   Antarctica   Asia
Australia   South America   Europe
Africa

1._____

2._____

3._____

4._____

5._____

6._____

7._____

From *Helping Your Child with Maps & Globes* published by Good Year Books. Copyright © 1994 by Bruce Frazee and William Guardia.

How far is a City?

Concept: Location and distance.

Objective: Discriminate the difference between longest/shortest distance.

Materials: Large card and string.

Procedure:

1. Help children sing the song "A Hop, a Skip, and a Jump."
2. Draw a large map of your state on the ground outside, locating four major cities.
3. Choose four children, one for each city, and place a large card with the name of the city in front of each child.
4. Have children sing the song while the children with cards will move from city to city, while the rest of the class makes a circle around the map of your state.
5. Use a question to check for understanding. Example: Each hop, each skip, each jump equals one hundred miles, so:
    • If it is one hop, one skip, one jump from City 1 to City 2, what is the distance between them?
    • How far is City 3 from City 1?
    • How far is City 4 from City 1?
    • Which city is farthest from City 1?

Enrichment/Extension:

• If you make a round-trip from City 1 to a City 4, how many miles would you have driven?

• If you make a round-trip to each of the three cities from City 1, how many miles would you have to drive?

• If you drive from City 4 to City 2, stopping over in City 1, how many miles do you have to drive?

Directions for Worksheet: Have children learn the song before doing the worksheet. Substitute the correct cities for your state.

From *Helping Your Child with Maps & Globes* published by Good Year Books. Copyright © 1994 by Bruce Frazee and William Guardia.

A Hop, a Skip and a Jump

Words by William Guardia Arranged by Mary Esther Bernal

From *Helping Your Child with Maps & Globes* published by Good Year Books. Copyright © 1994 by Bruce Frazee and William Guardia.

From *Helping Your Child with Maps & Globes* published by Good Year Books. Copyright © 1994 by Bruce Frazee and William Guardia.

A Hop, a Skip and a Jump

From San Antonio to Dallas
A hop, a skip, and a jump.
From San Antonio to Houston
Only a hop and a skip.

El Paso to San Antonio,
A hop, a skip, a jump,
And another hop and skip.

Let us hop around Texas.
Hopping, hopping, hopping,
Hopping, hopping, hopping.
Let us hop around Texas.
Hopping, hopping, hopping,
Hopping, hopping, hopping.
Let us hop around Texas, all day long.

Let us skip around Texas.
Skipping, skipping, skipping,
Skipping, skipping, skipping.
Let us skip around Texas.
Skipping, skipping, skipping,
Skipping, skipping, skipping.
Let us skip around Texas, all day long.

Let us jump around Texas.
Jumping, jumping, jumping,
Jumping, jumping, jumping.
Let us jump around Texas
Jumping, jumping, jumping,
Jumping, jumping, jumping.
Let us jump around Texas, all day long.

Where is my Continent?

Concept: Location of continents.

Objective: Locate each continent on a world map.

Materials: Colored circles of the continents.

Procedure:

1. Select seven children and assign each a continent.
2. Give each child a large colored circle with the name of a continent.
3. Locate the continents on a world map and a globe.
4. Give each child a copy of the "rap" verse. Go over the verse to set the rhythm and familiarize children with the words.
5. Give each child a few lines to recite in "rap" fashion.
6. Have children recite their rap lines. Have children with the name of the continent put their circle on the correct location on the wall map when the continent is introduced in the "rap" verse.

Enrichment/Extension: Allow the children to compose rap verses for other map reading concepts that have been studied in other lessons.

Directions for Worksheet: Duplicate enough copies to give to each child.

From *Helping Your Child with Maps & Globes* published by Good Year Books. Copyright © 1994 by Bruce Frazee and William Guardia.

Where is my Continent?

Directions: Learn the rap below.

1st Child:	North America is a continent.
Group 1:	North America is not a city.
	North America is not a country.
	North America is not a state.
All Children:	North America is a continent.
2nd Child:	South America is a continent.
Group 2:	South America is not a city.
	South America is not a country.
	South America is not a state.
All Children:	South America is a continent.
3rd Child:	Africa is a continent.
Group 3:	Africa is not a city.
	Africa is not a country.
	Africa is not a state.
All Children:	Africa is a continent.
4th Child:	Europe is a continent.
Group 4:	Europe is not a city.
	Europe is not a country.
	Europe is not a state.
All Children:	Europe is a continent.
5th Child:	Asia is a continent.
Group 5:	Asia is not a city.
	Asia is not a country.
	Asia is not a state.
All Children:	Asia is a continent.
6th Child:	Antarctica is a continent.
Group 6:	Antarctica is not a city.
	Antarctica is not a country.
	Antarctica is not a state.
All Children:	Antarctica is a continent.
7th Child:	Australia is a continent.
Group 7:	Australia is not a city.
	Australia is not a country.
	Australia is not a state.
All Children:	Australia is a continent.

From *Helping Your Child with Maps & Globes* published by Good Year Books. Copyright © 1994 by Bruce Frazee and William Guardia.

What are Latitude and Longitude?

Level 1

Concept: Latitude lines locate north and south. Longitude lines locate east and west.

Objective: Identify latitude lines as those that are north and south, on a grid they are drawn east and west. The longitude lines are those that are east and west, on a grid they are drawn north and south.

Materials: Globe, wall map, and butcher paper.

Procedure:

1. Locate the equator (O° latitude). Locate other latitudes. Ask: Which direction do we move (north and south)? Locate the prime meridian (O° longitude). Locate other longitudes. Ask: Which direction do we move (east and west)?

2. On a piece of butcher paper, make a simple grid system which would represent streets in a city.

Example:

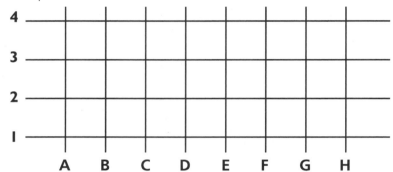

3. Ask questions such as if you travel north two blocks on Longitude Street B, how many Latitude blocks did you pass? What is the name of the intersection where you stopped? This helps children make the transition from a grid to latitude and longitude.

4. Use various maps to locate places by giving children latitude and longitude degrees.

Enrichment/Extension: Let children draw a city and make a grid overlay using latitude and longitude. Have children locate various places on their maps using their grid system.

Directions for Worksheet: Have children look at the map and answer the questions.

From *Helping Your Child with Maps & Globes* published by Good Year Books. Copyright © 1994 by Bruce Frazee and William Guardia.

Directions: Look carefully at the map and answer the questions. What symbol is located at:

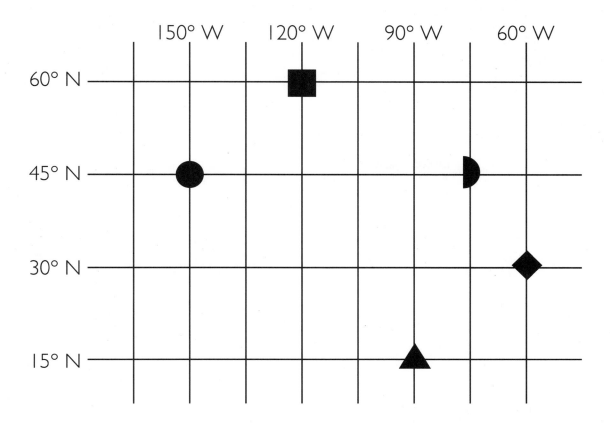

1. 45° N Latitude, 150° W Longitude?_____

2. 60° N Latitude, 120° W Longitude?_____

3. 15° N Latitude, 90° W Longitude?_____

4. 30° N Latitude, 60° W Longitude?_____

5. 45° N Latitude, 75° W Longitude?_____

Level 1

Concept: Locating positions with latitude and longitude.

Objective: Plot various locations using latitude and longitude.

Materials: Globe and maps with latitude and longitude lines, chalk or masking tape.

Procedure:

1. Review the concept of a grid. Show the relationship of a grid to the lines of latitude and longitude.

2. Put nine sheets of paper on the floor as shown:

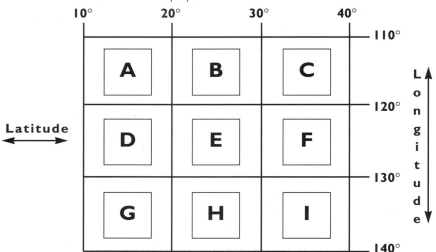

With chalk or masking tape, draw lines across (horizontally) to show latitude.
Draw lines up and down (vertically) to show longitude.
Write a letter on each sheet of paper as shown above.

3. Have children stand on various degrees of latitude and longitude and state their position by letters.
For example: 20° Latitude and 130° Longitude.
Answer: Between letters D and E.

4. Allow children to move to the locations while others observe.

Enrichment/Extension: Use 15°, 25°, 35° Latitude and 115°, 125°, 135° Longitude for the floor grid in this lesson. Explain that latitude and longitude do not always meet at the exact lines. For example: 25° Latitude and 135° Longitude would be the letter H. Allow children to practice plotting various locations.

Directions for Worksheet: Tell children they will practice plotting several locations on a worksheet. Do the first question to show as an example.

From *Helping Your Child with Maps & Globes* published by Good Year Books. Copyright © 1994 by Bruce Frazee and William Guardia.

Plotting Latitude and Longitude

Directions: Put a dot on the six locations given below. Connect each location and then draw what you see below the grid.

Locations

1. 40° N Latitude
   90° W Longitude

2. 30° N Latitude
   80° W Longitude

3. 20° N Latitude
   70° W Longitude

4. 40° N Latitude
   70° W Longitude

5. 30° N Latitude
   80° W Longitude

6. 20° N Latitude
   90° W Longitude

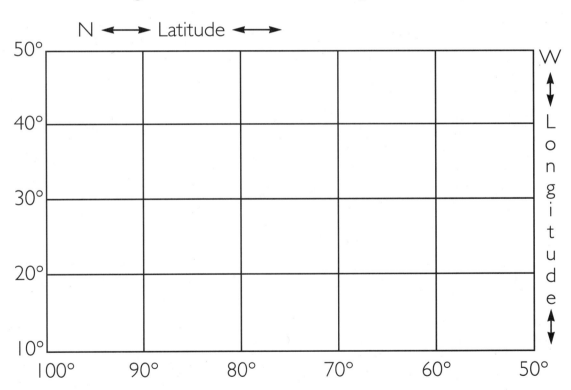

Drawing: What do you see?

From *Helping Your Child with Maps & Globes* published by Good Year Books. Copyright © 1994 by Bruce Frazee and William Guardia.

Where are Places in the Home?

Concept: Locating areas in a home.

Objective: Create a floor plan map of their ideal home.

Materials: Paper strips 1/2" × 12".

Procedure:

1. Show different homes, floor plans cut from magazines, or bring in actual blue prints, etc.
2. Discuss what people do in their homes (eating, sleeping, bathing, entertaining, etc.)
3. Instruct the children to think of their own family. Consider the living needs of the family based on: size, hobbies, ages; also, consider traffic patterns in the house.
4. Have children arrange paper strips (12" × 1/2") on a 12" × 18" sheet of paper. The strips represent the walls of the home. The spaces between represent the rooms. By positioning the pre-cut strips, the child can create a floor plan suited to the child's concept of the ideal home. Encourage pupils to experiment with many designs before gluing down the strips.
5. Label the appropriate rooms, such as living room, kitchen, bathroom, etc.
6. Make symbols and items from construction paper to represent home objects like: beds, television, stove tables, chairs, etc.

Enrichment/Extension: Invite an architect into the class to discuss residential design and drafting. Groups of children could design a commercial building such as a school, department store, factory, etc.

Directions for Worksheet: Have children read directions. Emphasize the location of the doors and windows while children design their house.

From *Helping Your Child with Maps & Globes* published by Good Year Books. Copyright © 1994 by Bruce Frazee and William Guardia.

Where are Places in the Home?

Directions: Look at the outline of this house. Draw lines to show where you would locate the living room, bathroom, kitchen, bedrooms, and hallways.

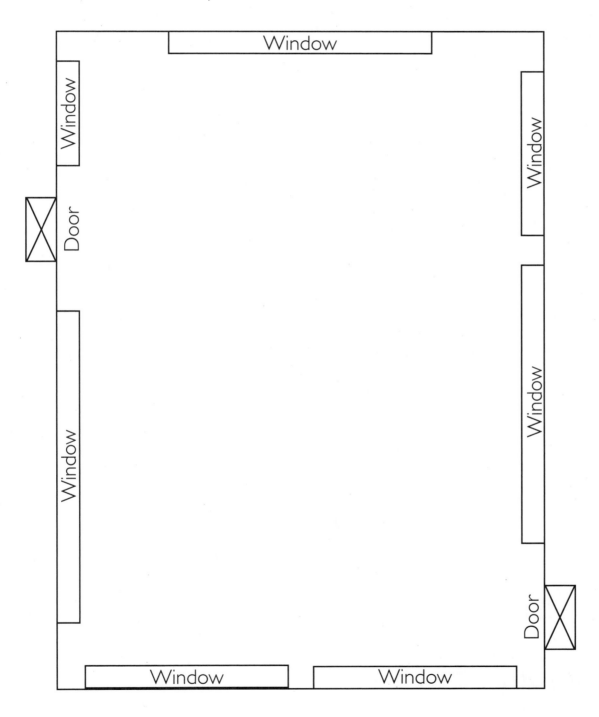

From *Helping Your Child with Maps & Globes* published by Good Year Books. Copyright © 1994 by Bruce Frazee and William Guardia.

Level 2

Concept: Locate places around the school neighborhood.

Objective: Describe the location of their home or school in relationship to the immediate environment around the school.

Materials: Mural paper or bulletin board paper, magic markers, and construction paper.

Procedure:

1. Discuss the streets that surround your home or school. Then note the cardinal directions, the names of all streets, and the location of notable landmarks such as the school, church, store, park, etc.
2. Plot these streets on a large sheet of mural paper.
3. Draw or put a picture of your home or school on the mural.
4. Write the cardinal directions and the location of several notable landmarks such as a park, store, etc.
5. Assign children to cut out particular neighborhood items from construction paper, such as stores, houses, trees, stop signs, etc.
6. Have each child glue these neighborhood items in the correct location on the mural map.

Enrichment/Extension: Discuss the mural map in terms of your home or school and use cardinal directions to reinforce the location of places in the neighborhood with respect to neighboring streets or landmarks.

Directions for Worksheet: Review the location of major landmarks near the school. Discuss whether these places are north, south, east, or west of the school. Have children locate and draw these on the worksheet.

From *Helping Your Child with Maps & Globes* published by Good Year Books. Copyright © 1994 by Bruce Frazee and William Guardia.

What is a Neighborhood Map?

Directions: What is around our school? Draw the things that are near our school. For example: buildings and bus stops. Color your drawing.

What is a Community?

Concept: To locate various landmarks and buildings in a community.

Objective: Locate various places on a single map.

Materials: Bulletin board paper, outline maps, and index cards.

Procedure:

1. Obtain a large sheet of bulletin board paper.
2. Draw (outline shapes) a small community on paper or use the worksheet that accompanies this lesson.
3. Prepare the index cards with specific questions like:
a. What symbol shows the school?
b. You work at a gas station. What is the symbol of the gas station?
c. Which direction do you go from school to work?
d. The river is on which side of town?
4. Put children in small groups, allowing the children to work on the index cards as they view the community map. Provide an answer sheet for each group.
5. Use a toy car as a way for the children to drive about the community to seek answers to the questions on the index cards.
6. Periodically index cards can be added to meet new map reading concepts taught.

Enrichment/Extension: Instead of drawing objects on the large bulletin board paper, a small community could be constructed from boxes or milk containers that can be used to represent the various stores, houses, etc. A street map would need to be made in order to locate places and answer questions on the index cards.

Directions for Worksheet: Have the children study the map and the map key. Then, answer the questions.

From *Helping Your Child with Maps & Globes* published by Good Year Books. Copyright © 1994 by Bruce Frazee and William Guardia.

What is a Community?

Directions: Answer the following questions.

1. Who lives across the street from the school?

  Bruce   Felicia   William

2. The City Park is between which streets?

  A and B Streets   B and C Streets   A and C Streets

3. How many stores are on the map?

  0   1   2   3   4   5

4. As you face William's house, in which direction is the church?

  North   East   West

5. How many streets go north and south?

  2   3   4

6. Which street would Bruce take to school?

  Main Street   A Street   South Street

7. Who's house is south of Main Street?

  Bruce's   Felicia's   William's

8. Draw some trees on the empty lots on South Street. Use the symbol for trees in the key.

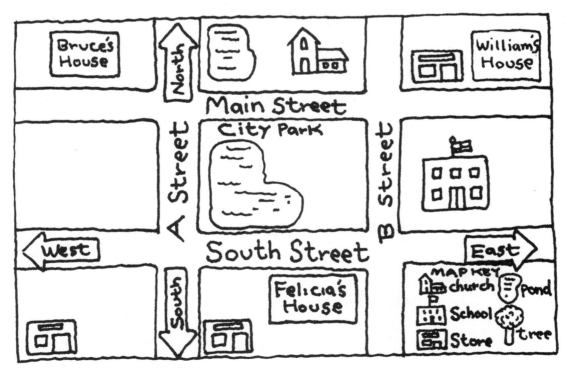

From *Helping Your Child with Maps & Globes* published by Good Year Books. Copyright © 1994 by Bruce Frazee and William Guardia.

From Here to Where?

Concept: Deciding the expense of travel in the United States.

Objective: Plan a vacation by car to a chosen destination using a specified amount of money.

Materials: Maps, vacation information, and travel agent brochures.

Procedure:

1. Obtain state and/or U.S. maps.
2. Explain that the map is to help plan for a weekend trip to a city of their choosing. They will need to budget and plan for:
   a. travel routes
   b. travel expenses
   c. expected departure and arrival dates
   d. lodging expenses
   e. food
   f. entertainment
   g. other items as decided by child groups
   h. three things to do at the city.
3. Phone or write to several motels and ask them to send you room rates, menus, and other available information.
4. Put the children into groups of 4-6 children. Allot each group a specified sum of money. Give two groups the same sum of money in order to make comparisons to those with equal and unequal sums of money.
   For example: Group A $500
   Group B $300
   Group C $200
   Group D $200
5. Place a time limit on the groups' work, stressing that each group should travel the best way with the fewest miles.
6. After children have planned their trips, allow for short debriefing sessions so each group can defend its excursion and budget.

Enrichment/Extension: Each group can design a poster about its trip. Have each group report trips by role-playing a travel agent trying to sell the others on the trip.

Directions for Worksheet: Have the children fold the paper at the perforated lines so directions are on the back side of the paper. Allow children to create a travel brochure.

From *Helping Your Child with Maps & Globes* published by Good Year Books. Copyright © 1994 by Bruce Frazee and William Guardia.

From Here to Where?

Directions: Design a travel brochure. Include information about location, things to do, and expenses.

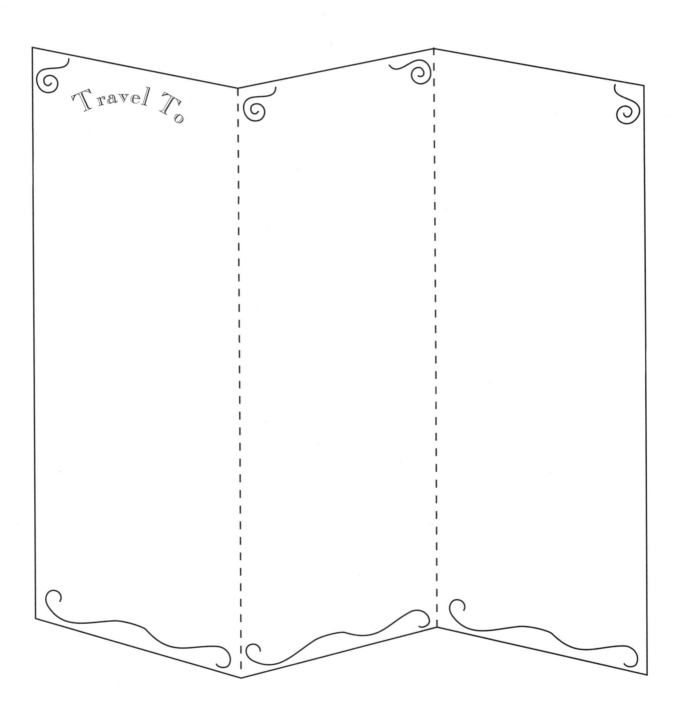

Travel To

What is a Treasure Hunt?

Concept: Follow directions to locate objects.

Objective: Interpret a map in order to locate an object hidden on the school grounds.

Materials: A treasure object, like a bag of candy coins, and an outline map of school grounds with landmarks.

Procedure:

1. Prepare a listing of various landmarks on the school grounds such as trees, swings, etc. Prepare a map of the school grounds. Show the cardinal direction north.

2. Hide a specified object on the school grounds. Number and hide several sequential directions that children would need to find in order to locate the specific object. The hidden directions should be located with each reference to the landmarks on the map.

3. Designate several groups for this activity and give each group member a map.

4. Go outside to practice pointing to and moving towards the various cardinal directions.

5. Explain to the children that they will have to use the map to find hidden pieces of information which will help them to discover the hidden object. Stress that each clue must be followed in order and that the directions must be put back where they were found.

6. Stagger the starting times so each group will have the opportunity to interpret and apply their directional skills based on the directions you have hidden. Be sure to tell the groups that the treasure will be equally shared by all regardless of who finds it first.

Enrichment/Extension: Allow the same child groups to construct their own treasure map and hide an object. Maps are exchanged and each group must locate the object by interpreting directions.

Directions for Worksheet: Have children locate and circle the hidden words.

From *Helping Your Child with Maps & Globes* published by Good Year Books. Copyright © 1994 by Bruce Frazee and William Guardia.

What is a Treasure Hunt?

Directions: Locate and circle these words that are in the puzzle below:

NORTH   TREASURE   SOUTH   MAP
EAST   LOCATE   WEST   DIRECTIONS

A	E	I	M	Q	U	Y	E	C	F	J	M	P	D
Q	T	W	A	E	I	R	N	R	U	Q	M	S	H
Y	D	D	I	Q	U	N	X	P	H	C	X	V	L
R	A	I	J	S	N	O	A	T	M	E	O	Z	P
J	F	R	A	I	V	R	H	G	X	V	I	D	T
E	O	E	U	W	U	T	F	A	U	G	N	S	T
Z	R	C	J	T	R	H	E	M	E	Z	A	H	X
T	Y	T	S	I	B	D	G	C	T	E	W	L	B
V	B	I	D	C	B	K	L	J	L	H	S	P	I
S	K	O	Y	O	N	H	J	F	D	S	F	K	O
O	Z	N	M	A	P	E	I	A	I	K	J	L	L
J	B	S	O	U	T	K	L	M	A	S	R	O	H
F	A	P	Q	O	W	X	Z	D	Y	F	I	C	E
B	Q	S	U	T	J	Y	G	X	K	H	Q	A	A
X	R	P	V	R	S	O	U	T	H	L	E	T	W
W	L	O	S	Z	U	V	W	Z	M	P	R	E	S
E	X	C	M	T	C	N	N	O	W	L	V	G	O
S	Y	B	G	K	P	D	Q	H	D	T	M	C	K
T	A	F	K	S	C	U	L	G	B	W	T	Y	G
B	F	J	N	R	V	Z	D	G	K	N	R	U	C

What are Some Famous World Cities?

Level 2

Concept: Locating cities on a world wall map.

Objective: Locate specific world cities.

Materials: Wall map and globe.

Procedure:

1. Put up a large world map in front of the class.
2. Locate and list 10 well-known world cities, such as Paris, Rome, Hong Kong, Beijing, Jerusalem, etc. Tell children that the class will go on a make-believe tour around the world.
3. Divide the class into 6 groups. Each group is allowed to go to the wall map and select one of the ten cities listed on the chalkboard.
4. After each group has selected its city, the teacher hands out the lesson worksheet, World Famous City Fact Sheet.
5. The groups will verify information using desk maps, encyclopedias, textbooks, or an atlas.

Enrichment/Extension:

1. Children locate their city on the globe. Have them determine what time it would be in that city. Have children locate latitude and longitude.
2. Have children think about what items they might need to travel to their city. What special conditions exist that are different than the city where they live?

Directions for Worksheet: Hand out the worksheet. Review and discuss major land areas using a world map and globe. Put children into groups. Let children use maps, globes, atlases, and encyclopedias to locate information on worksheet.

From *Helping Your Child with Maps & Globes* published by Good Year Books. Copyright © 1994 by Bruce Frazee and William Guardia.

World Famous City Fact Sheet

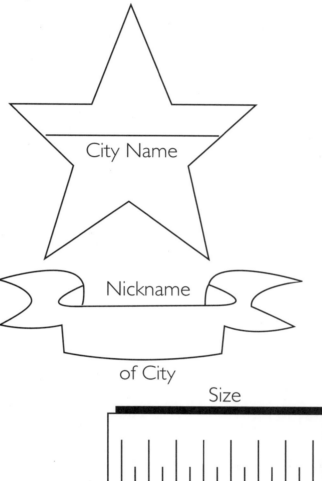

City Name

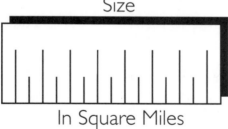

Nickname

of City

Industries

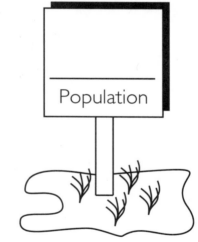

Population

Size

In Square Miles

Four interesting facts:

1. _____

2. _____

3. _____

4. _____

Facts collected by: _____

From *Helping Your Child with Maps & Globes* published by Good Year Books. Copyright © 1994 by Bruce Frazee and William Guardia.

Where do People Spend Money?

Level 2

Concept: Businesses are located near many people.

Objective: Analyze practical locations for businesses.

Materials: City maps, phone book, and large sheets of paper.

Procedure:

1. Discuss and list factors that influence the location of a business (traffic flow, population, zoning, other businesses, etc.)
2. Hand out maps of your area. Discuss the location of businesses found near the school or some other commonly known area. Use maps and phone books to locate areas and businesses.
3. Have children plan and map out an ideal city that demonstrates their ability to locate the plan areas for: businesses, housing, industries, public services, parks, etc. (See worksheet.)
4. On the back of the map have the children write or draw a story about their city and why it is good to live in that city.

Enrichment/Extension: For younger children, use manipulative blocks and/or toy houses, cars, etc. to lay out and create their city. For older children, obtain various maps from city planning to use and zoning as a basis for discussion laws related to economic growth.

Directions for Worksheet: Discuss businesses that are necessary for a community (grocery stores, clothing stores, building stores, etc.) and needed utility businesses (water, gas, electricity, etc.), as well as helpful service businesses (banks, gas stations, repair shops, etc.). Make a list of the top ten businesses needed for a community. Then have children complete the worksheet.

Where do People Spend Money?

Directions: Take the list of the top ten businesses needed by a community. Locate these on the map below. Think of reasons for your locations. Be sure to make a map key.

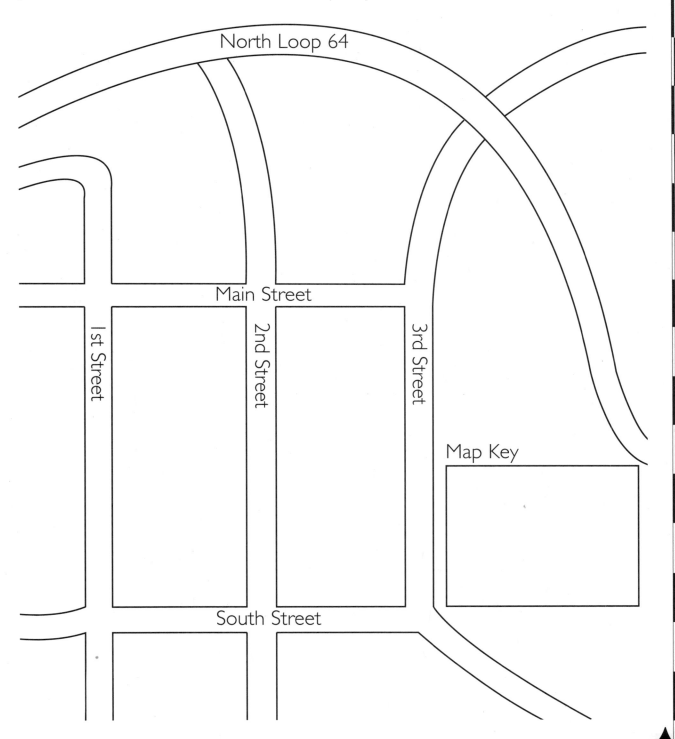

North Loop 64

Main Street

1st Street

2nd Street

3rd Street

Map Key

South Street

Level 2

Concept: Locate an area using a grid system.

Objective: Locate an area by following the numbers and letters of a grid system.

Materials:
Transparencies and colored markers.

Procedure:

1. Discuss the term "grid" and demonstrate on the chalkboard or overhead projector how numbers and letters on a grid help to locate a specific square.
2. Place a transparency with a grid system over a map transparency. Have children locate the number and letter of specific places or projects located in that particular grid square.
3. Using the grid in the worksheet or similar ones, have children locate the correct square.
   For example: Using attached worksheet, color square A2 red and square B1 green.

Enrichment/Extension: Tape or draw a grid system on the playground or floor. Children can hop or jump to the correct square.

Directions for Worksheet: Use the chalkboard or overhead projector to lead children through completion of the grids.

From *Helping Your Child with Maps & Globes* published by Good Year Books. Copyright © 1994 by Bruce Frazee and William Guardia.

Directions: Color the squares:

A1 – Yellow	A2 – Purple
C2 – Blue	B1 – Orange
D1 – Green	D2 – Black
B2 – Red	C1 – Brown

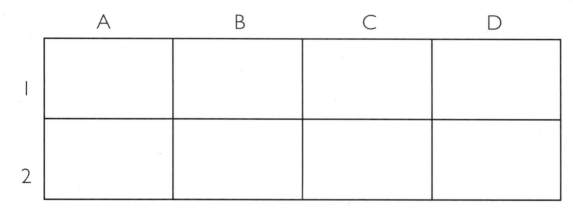

Write each letter in the correct square:

U – B2

R – E5

P – C3

S – A1

E – D4

From *Helping Your Child with Maps & Globes* published by Good Year Books. Copyright © 1994 by Bruce Frazee and William Guardia.

Where would You Build a City?

Concept: Identify various factors that lead to establishing a site for a city.

Objective: Evaluate various maps to make a decision about where you might locate a city and give reasons for decisions.

Materials: Pencils and duplicates of the worksheet.

Procedure:

1. Put children into groups. Give each group Map 1 of the worksheet. Explain they have just moved to this island to establish a new city. Their task is to locate the city and tell why they would pick this place for a city. Allow time for discussion and decisions. Have each group show and explain why they picked their locations.
2. Give children Map 2 of the worksheet and read the directions with them. Ask children if they would change the location of their city and why. Allow groups that changed their location time to show and explain their reasons for their change.
3. Repeat the same procedures, giving each group one map at a time to each group. Allow time for discussion and decisions. Permit groups that change locations to show and explain their reasons for their change.

Enrichment/Extension: Do this same activity, but use information from your state. Trace an outline map, vegetation map, rainfall map, elevation map and products map. Follow the same procedures for children to learn facts about their state using the various maps that provide basic state information. Compare their locations to cities in the state.

Directions for Worksheet: Duplicate enough copies for each group of children. Be sure to hand out one map at a time and allow time for discussion.

From *Helping Your Child with Maps & Globes* published by Good Year Books. Copyright © 1994 by Bruce Frazee and William Guardia.

Where Would You Build a City?

Directions: Where would you locate a city on this map and why.
Put a dot where your city is located.

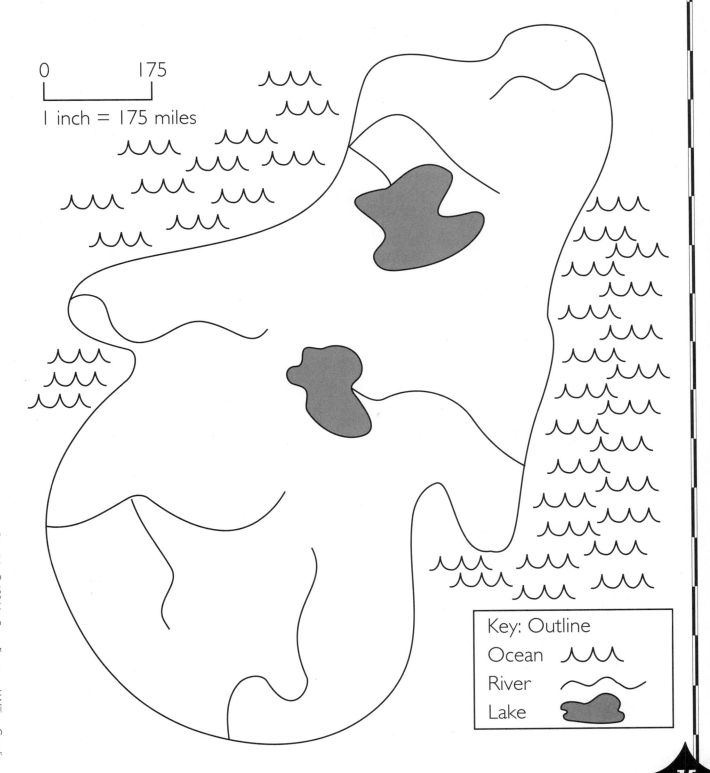

0   175

|———————————|

1 inch = 175 miles

Key: Outline
Ocean
River
Lake

Where Would You Build a City?

Directions: With the information on this map, would you change the location of your city? Put a dot on the same place if you did not change the location. Put an X in the new place if you changed the location of your city and tell why.

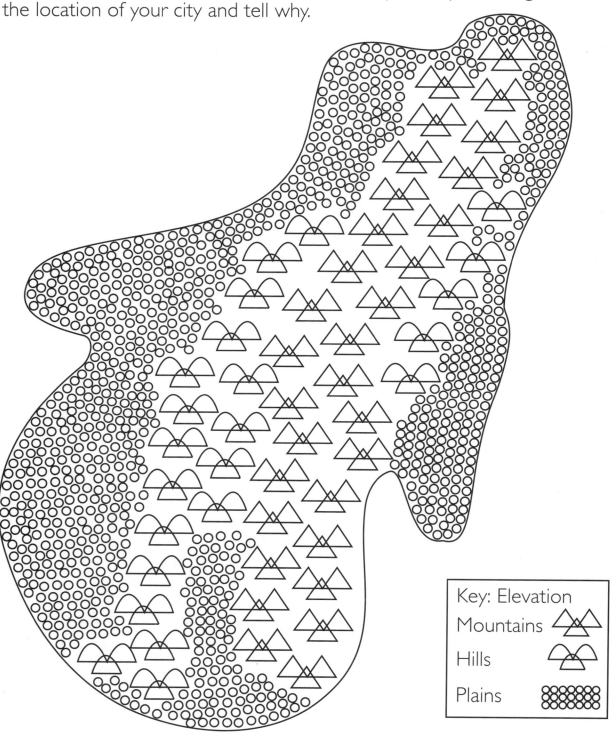

Key: Elevation

Mountains

Hills

Plains

From Helping Your Child with Maps & Globes published by Good Year Books. Copyright © 1994 by Bruce Frazee and William Guardia.

Where Would You Build a City?

Directions: With the information on this map, would you change the location of your city? Put a dot on the same place if you did not change the location. Put a square in the new place if your changed the location of your city and tell why.

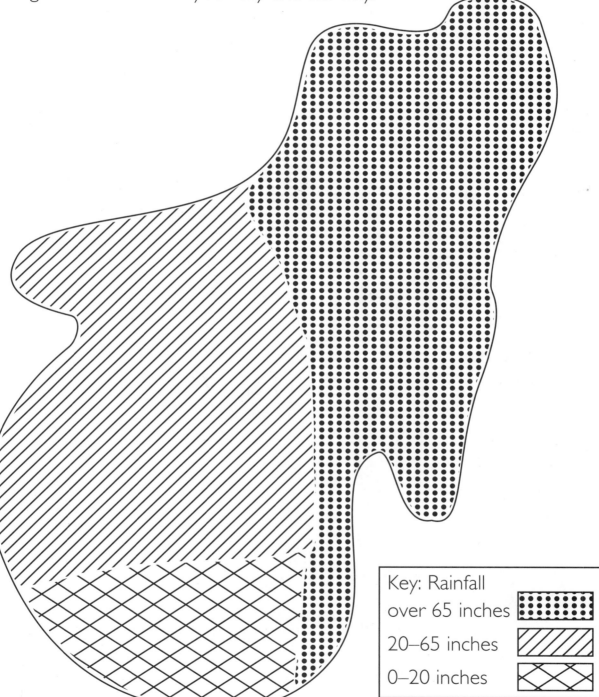

Key: Rainfall
over 65 inches
20–65 inches
0–20 inches

Where Would You Build a City?

Directions: With the information on this map, would you change the location of your city? Put a dot on the same place if you did not change the location. Put a circle in the new place if you changed the location of your city and tell why.

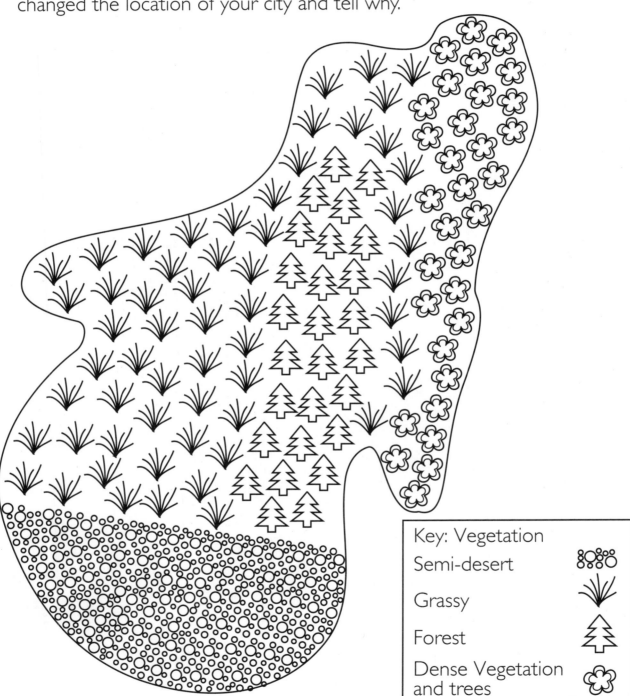

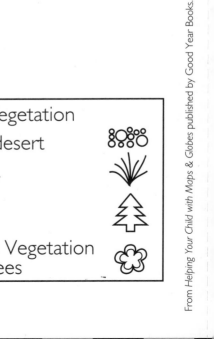

Key: Vegetation

Semi-desert

Grassy

Forest

Dense Vegetation and trees

Where Would You Build a City?

Directions: With the information on this map, choose the final location of your city and explain why you think it is a good location. Put a dot where your city will be and give it a name.

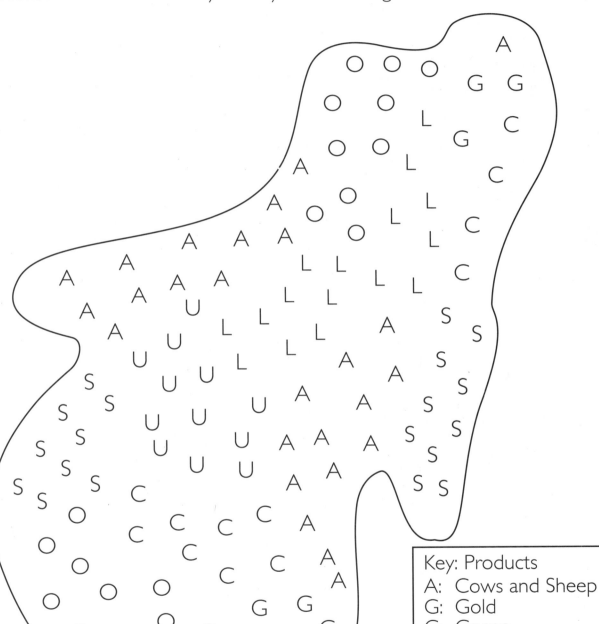

Key: Products
A: Cows and Sheep
G: Gold
C: Cocoa
U: Uranium
S: Silk
O: Oil
L: Lumber

Chapter Three: Direction

Teaching Children About Direction

Children must be able to orient themselves to north, south, east, and west in their immediate environment before they can understand cardinal directions. Learning about cardinal directions and developing skills that develop a child's sense of direction are basic to successful map interpretation.

Major emphasis in the early years should be on readiness experiences and familiarity with directional terms. Encourage children to use the term "up" as away from the center of the earth and "down" as toward the center of the earth. Use directional terms in routines and chores to make directions useful in everyday life. Constant use of directions helps to reinforce and build understanding.

The following activities will provide children with readiness skills before they begin the lessons that follow for this chapter.

1. Teach children basic positional words through movement and activity such as: up, down, around, above, below, sideways, front, and so forth.

2. Teach children directional words such as right and left and use them in giving directions to children. Say, "Put your toys into the box on your right." Use this technique with positional words as listed above.

3. Show children north, south, east, and west by using your home as a reference point. Use windows to show the sun coming in from the east and setting in the west of your home.

4. Purchase and show children how to use a compass.

5. Obtain a map of your town or city. Point out your street and house. Find the directions of other places in the area familiar to the children.

6. Create a treasure map of your backyard or playground. Choose a starting point and, on strips of paper, write directions for children to follow to find the treasure. Use directional and or positional words such as: two steps north, five steps toward the front of the house, and so forth.

7. Explore movement and direction by having children make their bodies "tall" (up) and "short" (down).

8. Use a toy car, doll, or other object to move around the room as children give directions such as: on top of the desk, down the side, in front of, to the left of, and other directional and positional words.

9. Play directional songs or games such as: Hokey Pokey, Simon Says, Follow the Leader, and Looby Loo to provide practice in direction and movement.

10. Develop a game by placing two separate objects in the playground or back yard, twenty feet apart. One represents the North Pole and the other represents the South Pole. Place children in the middle (draw a crossline representing the equator). Have children go up to the North Pole. Have child go down to the South Pole. Add other areas of the earth.

11. Walk children up a flight of stairs and back down a flight of stairs. Have children draw pictures of going up and coming down.

12. Take children out to the flag pole and have a flag raising ceremony (flag going up, flag going down). By the flag pole, draw a line from east to west. In the morning, have children point out where the sun is rising and predict where it is going.

13. Give children a map of their neighborhood and have them follow your directions: 1) Go from here to there by turning right only, and 2) Go from here to there by turning left only.

14. Take children, in a line, around the school or neighborhood. Lift your right hand and turn right, lift your left hand and turn left. Stop and have children look both ways, right and left, before crossing imaginary streets.

Skills to be Acquired: direction

1. Identifies cardinal direction.

2. Uses simple terms to describe direction (up-down, right-left, over-under).

3. Becomes familiar with the cardinal directions.

4. Uses right and left as direction.

5. Distinguishes between up and down and north and south.

6. Determines north and can orient self to the north direction.

From Helping Your Child with Maps & Globes published by Good Year Books. Copyright © 1994 by Bruce Frazee and William Guardia.

7. Understands that a map can help to determine the direction from one place to another.

8. States the direction of other objects in terms of north, south, east, and west.

9. Uses relative directions.

10. Determines the direction of other cities, states, countries, and continents.

11. Reads direction from maps oriented to north.

12. States the directions of objects using cardinal directions.

13. Uses the compass rose to determine directions.

14. Follows commands stated in cardinal directions.

15. Uses intermediate directions of northeast, northwest, southeast, and southwest.

16. Uses a grid system to determine direction.

17. Uses directions to get to a give place.

18. Finds north on a map.

19. Gives directions of other places from the United States, or a city in the United States.

20. Determines the direction of areas or places or a city or classroom map.

21. Understands that cardinal directions enable you to locate places.

From *Helping Your Child with Maps & Globes* published by Good Year Books. Copyright © 1994 by Bruce Frazee and William Guardia.

What is the Difference Between Up and Down?

Concept: Understand simple terms in following directions.

Objective: Discriminate between up and down.

Materials: A globe.

Procedure:

1. Ask children to look up at the lights, ceiling. Describe things that are "up."
2. Throw a ball into the air.
3. Discuss the terms up/down with regard to the motion of the ball.
4. Practice reinforcing this concept with heads up and heads down while children are at their seats.
5. Stress that "up" means away from the center of the earth and "down" means toward the center of the earth. Demonstrate this concept with a globe.

Enrichment/Extension: Direct children to clap their hands in front of themselves while humming a middle-toned sound. As the pitch of their voices rise, have them raise their hands above their heads. As the pitch of their voices lowers, have them lower their hands.

Directions for Worksheet: Give worksheet to children and read directions with children. Have children circle the direction they are taking, up or down.

From *Helping Your Child with Maps & Globes* published by Good Year Books. Copyright © 1994 by Bruce Frazee and William Guardia.

Difference Between Up and Down

Directions: Circle the direction you are taking, up or down, according to each sentence given.

1. This building has ten floors. If we are going from the fifth (5th) floor to the tenth (10th) floor, we are going:

   DOWN   UP

2. If we are going from the first (1st) floor to the sixth (6th) floor, we are going:

   DOWN   UP

3. From the ninth (9th) floor to the fourth (4th) floor, we are going:

   DOWN   UP

4. From the third (3rd) floor to the second (2nd) floor, we are going:

   DOWN   UP

5. If we are going from the third (3rd) floor to the seventh (7th) floor, we are going:

   DOWN   UP

Now that we know which direction we want to take, we can use the elevator!

Is it On or Over, Under or Around?

Concept: Understand simple terms in following directions.

Objective: Move over, under, around, and on a given object.

Materials: Rope and/or string.

Procedure:

1. Obtain a rope or string.
2. Have children go over and under the string.
3. Discuss other objects like bridges, tunnels, etc., that a person goes over or under.
4. Draw a large circle on the playground or floor. Ask children to go around the circle; step on the circle. Also teach terms such as: inside the circle, outside the circle.
5. Discuss other objects like trees, buildings, etc., that a person can go around or on.

Enrichment/Extension: Have groups of children, with a given length of string, describe what they do as they put the string over, under, around, and on various objects in the room.

Directions for Worksheet: Have children read the poem and use the illustration to identify what is on, over, under, or around and fill in the corresponding blanks.

From *Helping Your Child with Maps & Globes* published by Good Year Books. Copyright © 1994 by Bruce Frazee and William Guardia.

On, Over, Under or Around

Directions: Read the poem below. Look at the picture to find what is on, over, under, or around. Write in the blanks on, over, under, or around for each number in the picture.

I am on the water, riding my boat.
I go under the bridge, while you ride your bicycle over the bridge.
I am on a skateboard, going around the park and you take pictures of me.

1. _____   2. _____

3. _____   4. _____

5. _____

From *Helping Your Child with Maps & Globes* published by Good Year Books. Copyright © 1994 by Bruce Frazee and William Guardia.

Level 1

Concept: Understand simple terms in following directions.

Objective: Identify the directions left and right.

Materials: Verse of "Looby Loo," a substance with a nice smell, and water soluble markers.

Procedure:

1. Turn your back to the children and raise right hand. Say, "This is my right hand. Raise your right hand, touch your right ear, right toes, right knees." Point to the space on your side. Lean your body to the right. Mark each child's right hand with an "R." Use water soluble markers.
2. Repeat all activities with left hand.
3. Play the singing game "Looby Loo." Children stand in a circle and follow actions of song. Join hands on chorus and circle to the right.

Enrichment/Extension:

1. Use aftershave on the boys' right hands and perfume on the girls' left hands to reinforce left and right.
2. Use orange or lemon juice to mark the right hand to reinforce the concept of left and right.

Directions for Worksheet: Give worksheet to children and have them trace their way from ✗ to ★.

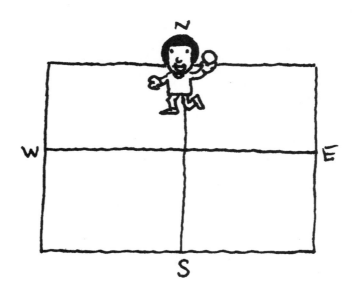

From *Helping Your Child with Maps & Globes* published by Good Year Books. Copyright © 1994 by Bruce Frazee and William Guardia.

Which is Left and Which is Right?

Directions: Start at the ✖ Here and trace your way to the ★.

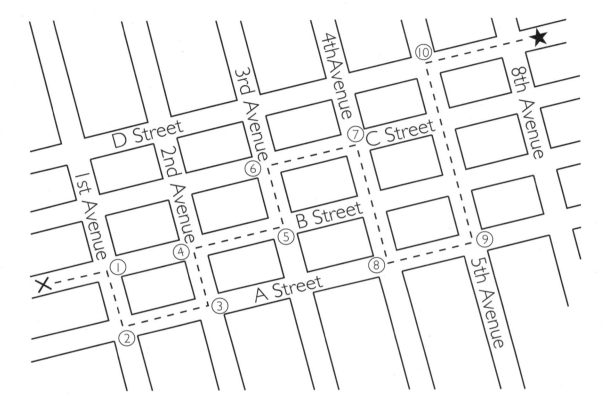

Which way do I turn at the circled number in order to get from ✖ to ★? Circle RIGHT or LEFT.

1. RIGHT—LEFT   6. RIGHT—LEFT

2. RIGHT—LEFT   7. RIGHT—LEFT

3. RIGHT—LEFT   8. RIGHT—LEFT

4. RIGHT—LEFT   9. RIGHT—LEFT

5. RIGHT—LEFT   10. RIGHT—LEFT

Are You Going Up or Down?

From *Helping Your Child with Maps & Globes* published by Good Year Books. Copyright © 1994 by Bruce Frazee and William Guardia.

Level 1

Concept: Locating using simple directions.

Objective: Define over, under, up, down, around, through, front, and back.

Materials: Chalkboard, drawing paper, story: Pang's Adventure, and a ping-pong ball.

Procedure:

1. Discuss the terms up, down, over, under, around, through, forward, and backward.

2. Show children a ping-pong ball and then read the story with blanks to be filled in as read by the class:
   There was once a little ping-pong ball named Pang. One day while Pang was being hit backward and forward across the ping-pong table, she decided enough was enough! She wanted to fly right through the window to see the world and that is just what she did! She bounced around the street, Pang saw a _____, but she bounced over it. Oh, oh. Pang almost rolled into a _____, but managed to squeeze under that. Pang bounced high. She bounced up the _____. She bounced down. She bounced over the _____, Presently, Pang spotted the tiniest little _____, but sped right around that; however, she ended up going right through the _____. She began to slow down. As she rolled up to the front of a silly looking _____, "My," she thought, "how strange that is." Just as Pang's movement began to slow, she found herself facing the back of a great big fat _____. "My goodness," Pang cried, "I certainly am happy out here in the big, wide world!"

3. Solicit responses from the class to fill in the blanks, writing the words on the board.

Enrichment/Extension: Children may role-play Pang's adventure, moving over, under, around, etc. the various objects stated in the story.

Directions for Worksheet: With the words provided on the worksheet, have children write sentences and illustrate each sentence in the space provided.

Are You Going Up or Down?

Directions: Write a sentence with each word given on the line next to each word. Draw a picture under the sentence you wrote.

1. Up: _____

2. Down: _____

3. Over: _____

4. Under: _____

5. Around: _____

6. Through: _____

7. Forward: _____

8. Backward: _____

Which Way is North?

Level 1

Concept: Orient the children towards north.

Objective: Identify the cardinal directions: north, south, east, and west.

Materials: Compass and paper.

Procedure:

1. Using a compass, locate the north wall of the classroom or room in your home. Pass the compass around, allowing each child to see how the marker points north.
2. Print North (or N) on a sheet of paper and place it on the north wall.
3. Do the same for the south, east, and west walls. Have children face the various directions as you call them out to practice orienting themselves to the correct direction.
4. Ask questions about the directions of other areas in the school or your home. For example: another teacher's room, cafeteria, playground, office, etc. Have children imagine they have x-ray vision to help them "see through" the walls.

Enrichment/Extension: Go outside and identify the cardinal directions. Practice facing the different directions. Identify objects within view as either being north, south, east, or west from where you stand while facing north.

Directions for Worksheet: Have children study the map. Identify the directions. Help children identify the direction of various places on the map from the area called "your classroom." Then have children answer the questions.

Which Way is North?

Directions: Look at the map and answer the questions below.

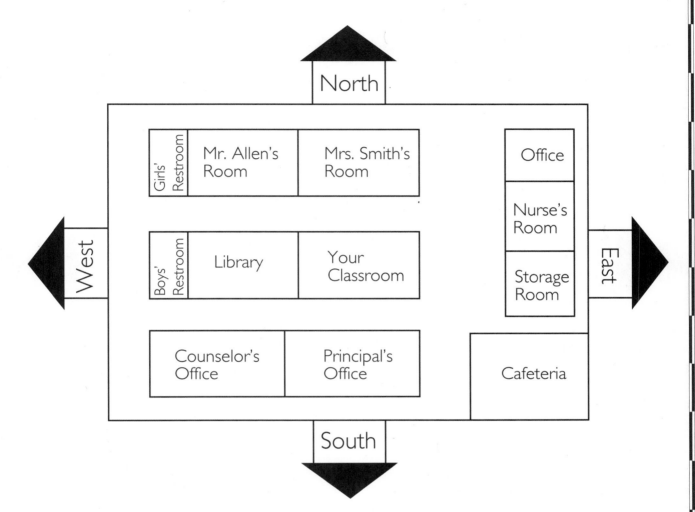

Fill in the blanks with North, South, East, or West.

1. Mr. Allen's Room is _____ of the Library.

2. The Library is _____ of the Nurse's Room.

3. Your classroom is _____ of the Boys' Restrooms.

4. The Principal's Office is _____ of Mrs. Smith's Room.

5. Your classroom is _____ of the Principal's Office.

Which Directions do I Take?

Concept: Follow cardinal directions.

Objective: Be able to move to towards the north, south, east, and west.

Materials: Nine cardboard boxes.

Procedure:

1. Position nine cardboard boxes of uniform size on the floor, three across and three down. These may represent city blocks and the floor space between them may represent streets. Choose a child to follow directions such as, "Move 2 blocks west, then 3 blocks south, then one block east," etc.

Enrichment/Extension: Divide the class into 2 teams. Have slips of paper on which are written a sequence of 4 directions such as:

1. Begin at the SW corner.
2. Go 2 blocks north.
3. Then 2 blocks east.
4. And one block south.

Score one point for each person who successfully completes the 4 direction sequence.

Directions for Worksheet: Have children answer the directional questions on the worksheet. For example: If I go from ▲ to ■, I am going 3 blocks west and 2 blocks south.

From *Helping Your Child with Maps & Globes* published by Good Year Books. Copyright © 1994 by Bruce Frazee and William Guardia.

Which Directions do I take?

Directions: Answer the questions below.

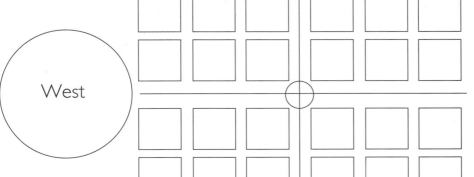

Fill in the blanks. For example: If I go from ▲ to ■, I am going 6 blocks west.

1. If I go from ● to ▲, I am going _____.

2. If I go from ■ to ▬, I am going _____.

3. If I go from ▲ to ●, I am going _____.

4. If I go from ▬ to ■, I am going _____.

5. If I go from ● to ■, I am going _____.

6. If I go from ▲ to ▬, I am going _____.

Level 1

Concept: Learn to follow cardinal directions.

Objective: Follow a given series of cardinal directions.

Materials: A series of cardinal directions on index cards.

Procedure:

1   Review the cardinal directions.
2.   Locate north using the compass.
3.   Divide children into several groups.
4.   Give each group a turn to follow a cardinal directions, such as:

   a.   Touch your elbow on the N wall.
   b.   Then put your knee on the W wall.
   c.   Write your name on the E wall. (Make sure this wall has a chalkboard.)
   d.   And go to the S wall and stop.

Enrichment/Extension: Introduce and give clues and actions for SE, SW, NE, and NW. Go outside and use directions to go through some physical exercises.

Directions for Worksheet: Have children illustrate the given objects in the correct circle or square.

From *Helping Your Child with Maps & Globes* published by Good Year Books. Copyright © 1994 by Bruce Frazee and William Guardia.

Am I Turning in the Right Direction?

Directions: Draw the objects named below in the correct circle or square.

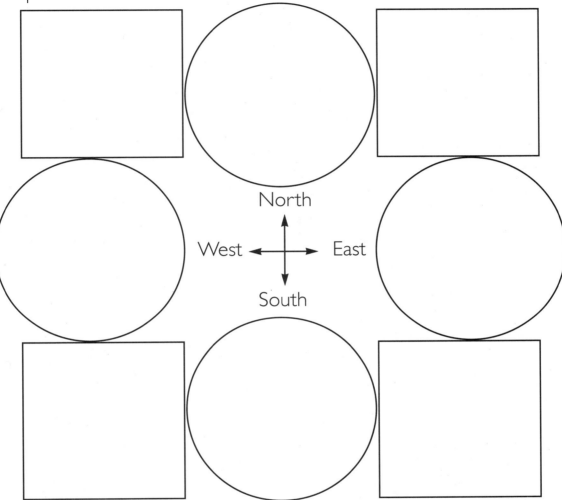

1. Draw a clown inside the NORTH circle.

2. Draw a school inside the EAST circle.

3. Draw a boat inside the WEST circle.

4. Write your name inside the SOUTH circle.

5. Draw a book inside the NORTHWEST square.

6. Draw a bird inside the SOUTHEAST square.

7. Draw a flower inside the NORTHEAST square.

8. Draw a car inside the SOUTHWEST square.

Level 1

Concept: Apply cardinal directions to a map of the United States.

Objective: Know the cardinal directions and learn a song.

Materials: Compass, outline map of the United States, and the song, "Walking, Looking."

Procedure:

1. Help children sing the song "Walking, Looking."
2. Draw a large outline map of the United States on the ground outside.
3. Take children outside and let them walk on the map and sing the song. First walk to the north, then walk to the south. Have children place their hands over their eyes and look either east or west as they sing the song.
4. Substitute various states in addition to Delaware and Maryland in the song.

Enrichment/Extension: Have children move to the area where states are located on the blacktop map. Discuss the direction these states are in relation to their own state.

Directions for Worksheet: Give children copies of the words. Practice singing the song before going outside.

From *Helping Your Child with Maps & Globes* published by Good Year Books. Copyright © 1994 by Bruce Frazee and William Guardia.

Walking, Looking

Words and music by William Guardia Piano arrangement by Mary Esther Bernal

Walk - ing,

walk - ing through the coun - try.

Look - ing

look - ing for a friend.

Walk - ing south, walk - ing north,

walk - ing all a - round.

Look - ing east, look - ing west,

peo - ple, peo - ple ev - ry - where_____.

*Children might be more comfortable singing an octave higher.

Walking, Looking

100

Walking, Looking

Walking, walking through the country.
Looking, looking for a friend.
Walking south, walking north, walking
  all around
Looking east, looking west,
People, people everywhere.

Walking, walking through the country.
Looking, looking for a state.
Walking south, walking north, walking
  all around.
Looking east, looking west,
Where's the state of Delaware?

Walking, walking through the country.
Learning, learning all about the land.
Walking south, walking north, walking
  all around.
Looking east, looking west,
Where's the state of Maryland?

From *Helping Your Child with Maps & Globes* published by Good Year Books. Copyright © 1994 by Bruce Frazee and William Guardia.

Level 1

Concept: Reinforce cardinal directions.

Objective: Be able to determine the direction a ball is thrown.

Materials: A ball.

Procedure:

1. Pick a child to use the compass and identify the cardinal directions and draw them on the playground. Pass the compass around and ask the other children to check if those directions are correct.
2. Tell children the ball represents the planet Earth.
   a. North, throw the planet Earth to the South.
   b. South, throw the planet Earth to the West.
   c. West, throw the planet Earth to the North.
   d. North, throw the planet Earth to the East.
   e. East, throw the planet Earth to the West.
3. Have as many groups of four children as the class size will allow play in the same game.
4. At first, children will follow directions and later one of the four children may be giving directions.

Enrichment/Extension: Break into groups of five children. One child monitors accuracy of the ability to follow the direction called out by the teacher. After a certain amount of time the group can compare scores.

Directions for Worksheet: Using the worksheet, have children identify the person in each square throwing the ball by writing the correct cardinal direction in the blank.

From *Helping Your Child with Maps & Globes* published by Good Year Books. Copyright © 1994 by Bruce Frazee and William Guardia.

Who is Throwing the Ball?

Directions: Find the person throwing the ball in each square by writing the correct cardinal direction the person is standing at in the blank.

1. _____

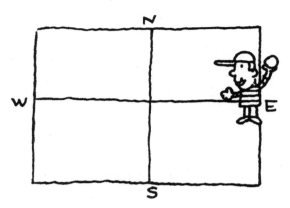

2. _____

3. _____

4. _____

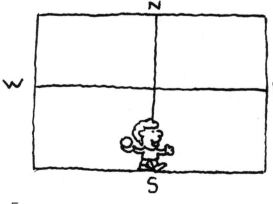

5. _____

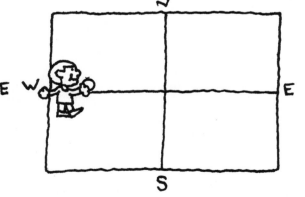

6. _____

What Size?

Concept: Compare various maps to form generalizations.

Objective: Compare the size of various maps of a country or state.

Materials: Outline map of states, textbook/atlas, and wall maps.

Procedure:

1. Give children a paper showing three differently sized outline maps of a state.
2. Ask children to draw another map of the same state.
3. Have children study the various maps in their textbook and, if possible, some wall maps.
4. Using a questioning strategy, help children further understand that people draw both small maps and large maps and this does not make the state smaller or larger.

Enrichment/Extension: Show the map key of each map and discuss the information found. Compare the amount of information on one map to a larger or smaller map of the same states or countries. Compare scales to compute size of state or country on each map.

Directions for Worksheet: Have children read the directions for the worksheet. Provide children with a copy of their state in order to illustrate a large, larger, and largest outline for the worksheet.

What Size?

Directions: Study the picture below. The circle represents a state.

LARGE   ⟶   ◯   ⟵   SMALLEST

LARGER   ⟶   ◯   ⟵   SMALLER

LARGEST   ⟶   ◯   ⟵   SMALL

Draw an outline of your state.

LARGE ⟶

LARGER ⟶

LARGEST ⟶

From *Helping Your Child with Maps & Globes* published by Good Year Books. Copyright © 1994 by Bruce Frazee and William Guardia.

What is a Compass Rose?

Concept: Intermediate directions.

Objective: To further understand the cardinal directions and begin to know the difference between north and northwest, south and southwest, etc.

Materials: Index cards.

Procedure:

1. Draw the outline of the figure shown on the worksheet on the ground in the playground with North facing true north.
2. Have eight children step on the eight spots. (The rest of the children may stand on the side and observe until their turn comes.)
3. Have children identify the area on which they are standing. Ex.: north; south; southwest, etc. Children standing on "N," "S," "E," or "W" should stand inside the line, and the teacher reinforces the cardinal directions. Children standing on an intermediate direction stand outside the line, and the teacher reinforces the term "intermediate direction."
4. Have each of the eight children call out their location and whether they are inside or outside of the lines.
   a. "I am inside the lines, I am North!"
   b. "I am outside the lines, I am Southwest!"
5. After each child has identified himself/herself, have children rotate clockwise and repeat.

Enrichment/Extension: Have eight cards in a box. Each card identifies an area "S," "N," etc. Pick a winner by picking one card. The winner will be identified as that area for one day, that is, he/she will be known as Mr./Ms. North until the next day. The winning child must name 5 facts concerning his/her location relative to the classroom, school, or state.

   a. In the northwest of the classroom there is a book, a globe, a door, a flag, and an aquarium.
   b. To the South of Ohio is Mexico, South America, the Gulf of Mexico, the cotton belt and many oil wells.

Directions for Worksheet: After identifying one cardinal direction, have children complete the remaining identifications and have them draw an object in each area.

From *Helping Your Child with Maps & Globes* published by Good Year Books. Copyright © 1994 by Bruce Frazee and William Guardia.

What is a Compass Rose?

Directions: Fill in the blanks with the correct cardinal directions, then draw an object in each area.

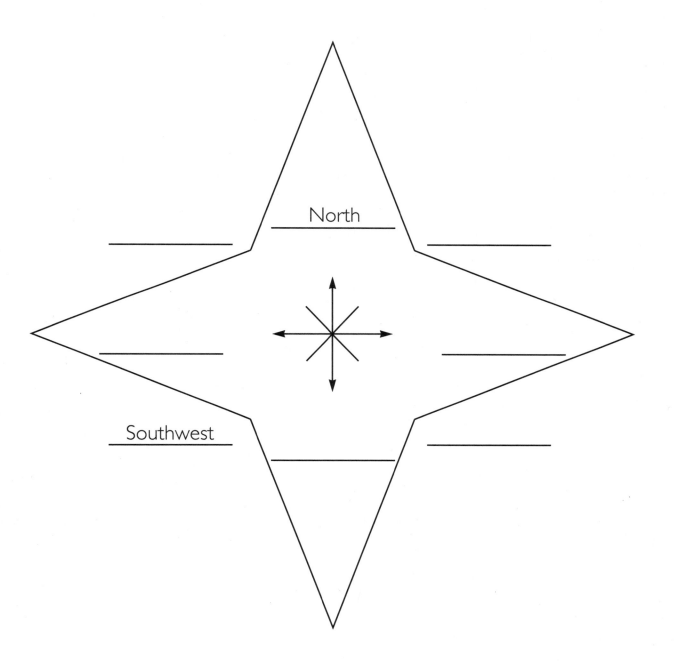

North

Southwest

What About the Lands of Ba and Tal?

Concept: Interpret information from two maps while constructing a map key.

Objective: Apply interpretation skills while comparing various features on several maps and constructing a map key.

Materials: Maps, markers, and 8 1/2" x 11" paper.

Procedure:

1. Have children write a creative paragraph about the Land of BA.
2. Give children a copy of the Land of BA taken from the top portion of the worksheet.
3. Give children five objects to place on the map. Have children create a symbol for each object and develop a map key.
4. Have children draw a picture of a person known as BAKING in the space provided on the worksheet.
5. The next day children will write a creative paragraph, the topic being the Land of TAL.
6. Give children a copy of the Land of TAL taken from the bottom portion of the worksheet.
7. Give children five objects to place on the map. Have children create a symbol and develop their own map key.
8. Have children draw a picture of a person known as TALKING in the space provided on the worksheet.

Enrichment/Extension: Give children an 8 1/2" x 11" paper on which children can draw a person known as TAL QUEEN. Have children create their own land and place objects in their map, creating symbols and a map key for each object.

Directions for Worksheet: Follow lesson plan as stated above.

From *Helping Your Child with Maps & Globes* published by Good Year Books. Copyright © 1994 by Bruce Frazee and William Guardia.

The Lands of Ba and Tal

The Land of Ba

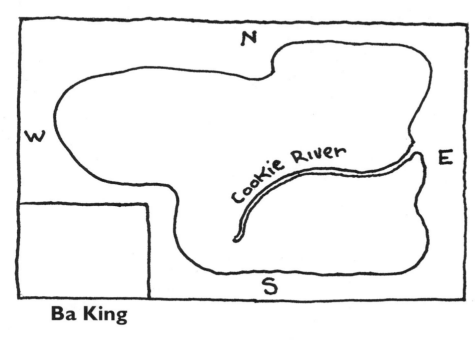

Ba King

Map Key

The Land of Tal

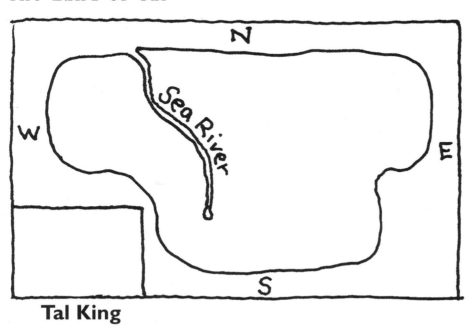

Tal King

Map Key

From *Helping Your Child with Maps & Globes* published by Good Year Books. Copyright © 1994 by Bruce Frazee and William Guardia.

Level 2

Concept: Determine cardinal directions.

Objective: Be able to locate areas between cardinal directions and to interpret information given in a map key.

Materials: Seating map, overhead projector (optional), transparency and worksheet.

Procedure:

1. Make a transparency of the worksheet to show on an overhead projector. Give a copy of the worksheet to children.
2. Reinforce the definition and purpose of a map key.
3. Give six questions to children:
   a. How many children are absent in the northeast area?
   b. How many children are present in the southwest area?
   c. Which area has the most children absent?
   d. How many children are present in all four areas?
   e. How many children are absent in both areas west of the line?
   f. Which area has the most children?
   g. How do you feel when you are absent?
   h. How do you feel when your best friend is absent?
   i. Why are children absent from school? Allow children to give several reasons.

Enrichment/Extension: At the end of the lesson, a bulletin board display can be made by the teacher or children showing a map of the classroom seating. The map should be divided into quadrants: NE, NW, SE, and SW. The class seating chart should also show children present, until each morning's attendance is taken and the absent symbol is added where appropriate.

Directions for Worksheet: Children may use their copy of the worksheet as an example of a map of a classroom. Ask children to make their own classroom map and map key, and record children present and absent for a week.

From *Helping Your Child with Maps & Globes* published by Good Year Books. Copyright © 1994 by Bruce Frazee and William Guardia.

Who is Absent?

Directions: Make your own classroom map and map key and record who is present and who is absent.

North

South

West — — — — — — — — — — — — — — — East

S S		S S
S S		S S
X S		S X

S S		X X
S S		S S
S S		S S

X S
Absent Present

Who Lives West of the River?

Concept: Compare information among maps.

Objective: Formulate generalizations and draw conclusions by comparing several maps.

Materials: Worksheet.

Procedure:

1. Give children a copy of the worksheet. Ask children the following questions:
   a. What is the population west of the river in Alpha State?
   b. Which of the three states has the largest population west of the river?
   c. What is the total population of Beta and Alpha States together?
   d. What is the total population west of the river of all three states?
   e. Is the population in Gamma State larger on the west side of the river or the east side of the river?
   f. Which of the states would you like to live in?

Enrichment/Extension: Give a name to each of the rivers and give names to each center of population.

Directions for Worksheet: Give each child a copy of the worksheet and ask the questions stated in the lesson. Children may select a state and add more information and develop a booklet giving the information about their respective state.

Who Lives West of the River?

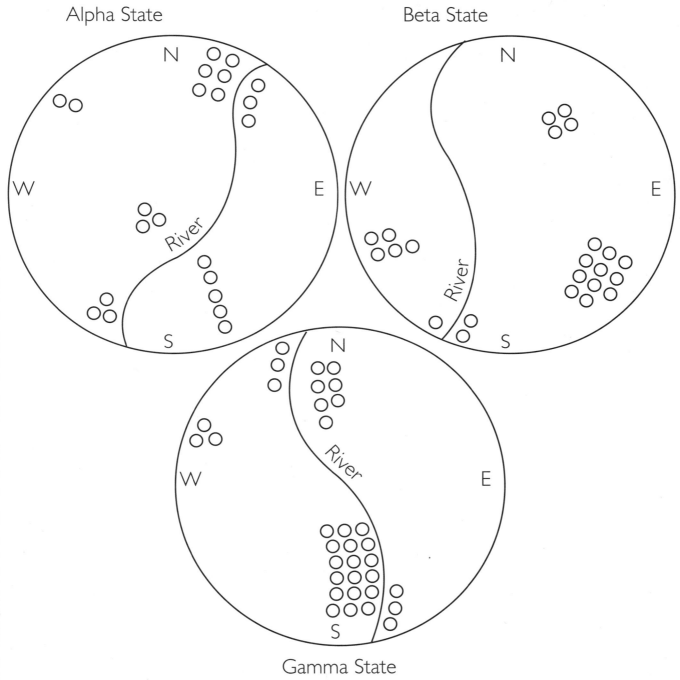

Alpha State

Beta State

Gamma State

Key:
○ = One Million People

Which Way is a State from my State?

Concept: Application of cardinal directions.

Objective: State relative directions of various places in the United States.

Materials: Outline maps.

Procedure:

1. Give children an outline map of the United States, including outline of states.
2. Have children fill in the following blanks with either north, south, east, or west.
   a. New York (NY) is _____ of Florida (FL).
   b. Texas (TX) is _____ of Michigan (MI).
   c. Louisiana (LA) is _____ of Montana (MT).
   d. Ohio (OH) is _____ of Mississippi (MS).
   e. Maine (ME) is _____ of California (CA).
   f. New Jersey (NJ) is _____ of Illinois (IL).
   g. Nevada (NV) is _____ of the Mississippi River.
   h. The Rocky Mountains are located _____ of the state of Washington (WA).
   i. North Carolina (NC) is _____ of South Carolina (SC).
   j. Indiana (IN) is _____ of Alabama (AL).

Enrichment/Extension: Give children relative directions for other geographical features in the United States.

For example:
   a. The Appalachian Mountains are _____ from the Mississippi River.
   b. The Great Lakes are _____ from the Gulf of Mexico.
   c. The Grand Canyon is _____ from the San Francisco Bay.

Directions for Worksheet: Have children write information about their state on the worksheet. Have them write the same information about another state they choose.

From *Helping Your Child with Maps & Globes* published by Good Year Books. Copyright © 1994 by Bruce Frazee and William Guardia.

Locating a State from my State

Directions: Fill in information about your state.

Alaska

WA
OR
ID
MT
ND
MN
WI
MI
ME
VT/NH
MA
CT RI
NY
PA
NJ
OH
DE
MD
WV
VA
Washington DC
SD
WY
NE
IA
IL
IN
NV
UT
CO
KS
MO
KY
NC
CA
AZ
NM
OK
AR
TN
SC
Hawaii
TX
LA
MS
AL
GA
FL

Our Country

Facts about my state:

1. Size: _____

2. Flower: _____

3. Capitol: _____

4. Population: _____

5. Major Industry: _____

6. Draw the flag below:

Facts about another state: _____

_____

_____

_____

From *Helping Your Child with Maps & Globes* published by Good Year Books. Copyright © 1994 by Bruce Frazee and William Guardia.

Chapter Four: Scale and Distance

Teaching Children About Scale And Distance:

The concept of scale and distance is very abstract and difficult for young children. Using scales involves the ability to estimate, find, and show real distances between points on the earth and given areas. Scale should be introduced at an early age so a child can begin to estimate how large an area is and infer distances between areas. Children can be taught about scale by comparing actual items to scale models as the idea that a map represents a real area greatly reduced in size is a difficult one for young children. Young children need to construct simple school and neighborhood maps. With these maps, the children can practice reducing the size of real objects so that the reductions become representations on their maps. When three-dimensional models (blocks, toy cars, or doll house furniture) are used, children can gain a better understanding of scale. To learn scale and its applications, parents and teachers need to begin with simple comparisons of ground and map distances. Mathematical computations of scale will likely be too advanced for most young children, so choose familiar objects to help estimate and show real distances.

The following activities will provide children with readiness skills before they begin the lessons that follow for this chapter.

1. Pour water or sand from a large container into a smaller container. Discuss scale in terms of large and small.

2. Discover various and arbitrary ways to show distance between two areas in a room or in the neighborhood by measuring body movements such as: hops, skips, jumps, sideway steps, slides, hands, feet, and so forth.

3. Use long and short pieces of string to measure the distance between two areas. Point out that distance was still the same even though you used different scales (long and short strings).

4. Make a map of a room on a standard sheet of paper. Compare the size of paper to the actual room.

5. Take a walk around the neighborhood or school, one block at a time. Ask children to take notes of the area. Upon returning, ask children to draw pictures of the area they just walked around. The next day, walk two blocks and repeat the activities. And the end of a week, ask children to draw pictures of one block, two blocks, three blocks, etc. and compare the pictures.

6. Using children's maps from #5 above, talk about what is near and what is far from home or school.

7. Have children interview parents, family, and friends about "What is a mile?" Walk a mile with the children. Drive a mile, then two miles, then three miles. Help children discover how long it takes to walk a mile and drive a mile.

8. Have a discussion on "How long does it take to walk or drive to school?" Include ideas about mileage, as discovered in #7 above, traffic, etc.

9. Have each child take five objects of various sizes and draw the objects to scale on a small piece of paper. Then place these objects on the floor and view through a small hole in a piece of paper and draw new views of objects on a piece of paper.

10. On a United States map, locate your city and five other cities in different states. Ask the question, "Which city is nearest to ours, which city is farthest?"

11. Take a photo of two children and show the class or group of children the real children and their photos. Explain the fact that the real children are much bigger then their photos, which make them look small.

Skills to be Acquired: Scale and Distance

1. Understands the relationship between smaller objects representing larger objects.

2. Compares sizes of cities, states, countries on several maps.

3. Knows that maps represent larger areas.

4. Uses various terms to express differences in relative size and distance.

5. Uses approximation and distance to represent scale.

6. Interprets the ratio of scale to actual distance or size.

From *Helping Your Child with Maps & Globes* published by Good Year Books. Copyright © 1994 by Bruce Frazee and William Guardia.

7. Uses objects to show relative scale difference between objects.

8. Describes distance using various terms such as right, left, up, down, over, under, and back, front.

9. Understands that objects vary in distance from one another.

10. Uses simple measurement to determine distances on a map.

11. Measures distances using various objects and converts those distances to a ratio and scale.

12. Understands that there is a difference in distance between various parts on a map.

13. Solves problems measuring distance indoors and outdoors and on maps and globes.

14. Interprets scale to determine distance.

15. Understands that time increases with distance.

16. Understands and computes distance and time.

17. Uses a highway map to detail distance, direction, location, time, and activities.

Post Office

House

School

Store

What is Near and What is Far?

Concept: Relative distance of objects.

Objective: Describe the distance of objects by using the terms near and far.

Materials: Index cards, colored construction paper, string, and an outline map of the United States.

Procedure:

1. Write the terms near and far (twice each) on four index cards. Pronounce and review the words for children.
2. Choose four children. Attach string to the index cards. Have children choose and wear an index card. Put "near" and "near" together and "far" and "far" apart. Define the concept of near and far by maneuvering the children about the classroom.
3. Distribute several different colored construction paper squares at various locations in the classroom. Ask children questions like:
   a. Which color square is near you?
   b. Which color square is far from you?
   c. Which color square is near a different colored square?
   d. Which color of square is far from a different colored square?
4. List specific places near and far from school. Have children identify the places listed as being near or far.

Enrichment/Extension: Using an outline map of the United States, locate your own state. Have children tell which state is near their own state and which state is far.

Directions for Worksheet: Point to the various places on the map. Do the first question with children. Read each question and point to the places for non-readers.

From *Helping Your Child with Maps & Globes* published by Good Year Books. Copyright © 1994 by Bruce Frazee and William Guardia.

Directions: Look at the map. Complete each sentence below. Fill in the box to the left of the correct answer.

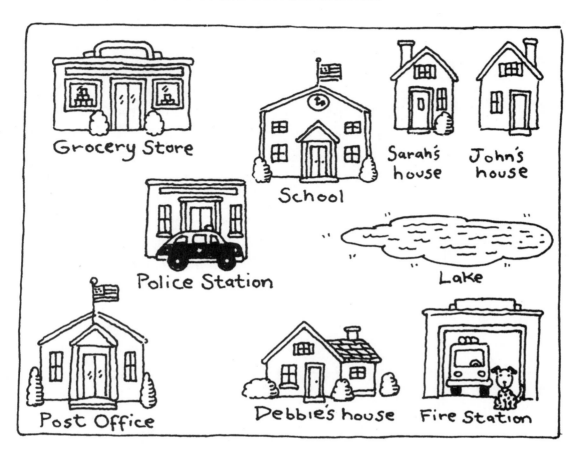

From *Helping Your Child with Maps & Globes* published by Good Year Books. Copyright © 1994 by Bruce Frazee and William Guardia.

1. Debbie's house is near the _____.

   grocery store   post office   John's house

2. The school is near _____.

   fire station   grocery store   Sarah's house

3. The fire station is near the _____.

   lake   police station   school

4. John's house is far from the _____.

   post office   school   lake

5. The grocery store is far from the _____.

   school   fire station   police station

What is Long and Short?

Concept: Distance between objects.

Objective: Compare the relationship of distance and time by using the terms long and short.

Materials: String, paper, and pencils.

Procedure:

1. Review measurement in terms of a foot and a yard.
2. Divide the class into groups and explain that each group will receive a piece of string. Some groups will receive a piece of string one foot long and another group will receive a piece of string one yard long.
3. Explain that each group must use the string to measure the distance around the classroom (length and width). Each group must count the number of times each piece of string is used to measure the distance.
4. Time the groups and appoint a counter for each group to mark the number of lengths of string that are used to measure the classroom. Start the groups in different corners of the classroom to minimize clustering.
5. Compare and discuss the differences between the group using the short string and the group using the long string. Discuss the relationship between distance and time. Describe examples of walking, bicycling, car, bus, train, and airplane. Point out the size of measurement, short string or long string, had an effect on the length of time even though the distance was the same.

Enrichment/Extension: Extend the measurement of the classroom by making a scale of 1 unit:1 foot. Assign a group of children to mark the dimension of a piece of bulletin board paper. Assign other groups to make scale items of select objects in the classroom to glue on the paper. Discuss and include symbols and a map key.

Directions for Worksheet: Explain to children that each group will receive a short piece of string (1 foot) and a long piece of string (1 yard). They must measure and draw a list of five objects that are shorter than one foot and five objects that are longer than one yard on the worksheet.

From *Helping Your Child with Maps & Globes* published by Good Year Books. Copyright © 1994 by Bruce Frazee and William Guardia.

What is Long and Short?

Directions: Draw or write the names of five objects in the classroom that are short (less than the shorter string) and five objects that are long (greater than the longest string). Put your answers in the space below.

Short   Long

1.   1.

2.   2.

3.   3.

4.   4.

5.   5.

The short string is one foot. The long string is one yard.

From *Helping Your Child with Maps & Globes* published by Good Year Books. Copyright © 1994 by Bruce Frazee and William Guardia.

What is a Mile?

Concept: Length of distance (a thousand paces).

Objective: Describe various ways to measure the approximate length of a mile.

Materials: None.

Procedure:

1. Draw one long line on the blackboard and divide it into ten sections.
2. Describe to the children that this line represents one mile and that each section represents one city block.
3. List ways in which children can measure one mile:
   a. by walking ten blocks with their parents.
   b. by riding a bicycle.
   c. by having parents drive their car around ten blocks.
   d. by going around a football field or playground a certain amount of times, depending on the length of the filed or playground.
   e. by counting the paces for one block and multiplying the number by ten.
   f. by timing how long it takes to walk a mile, ride a bicycle, etc.

Enrichment/Extension: Having the basic idea of what a mile is, children may design various ways to illustrate, on paper, what a mile is, and safety rules for walking, driving, riding.

Directions for Worksheet: Illustrate one way in which to find the length of a block or field. Then, have children draw circles, triangles, rectangles, squares, and describe ways they use to measure a mile.

From *Helping Your Child with Maps & Globes* published by Good Year Books. Copyright © 1994 by Bruce Frazee and William Guardia.

What is a Mile?

Directions: Answer the questions below.

One Mile

One Block

1. If you live 2 miles from school, how many blocks do you walk to get to school? _____

2. If your friend lives 5 miles from your house, how far would you have to walk to visit? _____

3. If your father drives 8 miles to the airport, how many blocks did he drive to get there? _____

4. If you rode your bike 10 blocks to the store, how many miles did you ride? _____

5. The annual parade in your city is 100 blocks long. If you march in the parade, how many miles will you march?_____

_____

What is Scale?

Concept: Map scale shows the real distance between places.

Objective: Define scale.

Materials: Ruler, pencils, maps and the globe.

Procedure:

1. Hold up a globe in front of the class and ask if it is the real earth. Let children explain differences between the globe and the real earth.
2. Explain that a globe is a smaller model of the earth. Real places are too large to fit on the globe.
3. Hand out the worksheet and discuss the scale drawings and questions with the children.
4. Explain that no matter what size a drawing is, the size of the object is the same. Scale helps you to find out the real size of an object as well as the distance between places.
5. Remind children to always look at the map key and the map scale. This lets them know what the real place on the map is like and how far or near objects (symbols) on the map are from one another.

Enrichment/Extension: Have children bring to school various scale models, such as trains, planes, cars, dolls. Discuss how the models are alike and different. Relate the models to the children's experience with real-life objects.

Directions for Worksheet: Look at the two drawings of the school bus. Explain that both show the same bus, however, each is drawn to a different scale. Discuss the two buses and answer the questions together in class.

From *Helping Your Child with Maps & Globes* published by Good Year Books. Copyright © 1994 by Bruce Frazee and William Guardia.

What is Scale?

Directions: Look at the two pictures of the school bus. Fill in the answers to the questions.

Drawing 1:

        1 inch = 10 feet

├————— 1 inch = 10 feet —————┤

Drawing 2:

        1 inch = 15 feet

├————— 1 inch = 15 feet —————┤

Drawing 1 is about 5 inches long. You have 5 groups of 10 feet or 50 feet in all.

Drawing 2 is about 4 inches long. You have 4 groups of 15 feet or 60 feet in all.

1. What is used to show the real size or distance of objects?

_____

2. How are the school buses alike/different?

_____

3. Why is one school bus smaller?

_____

4. Why are the real school buses the same size?

_____

Where is Scale on a Map?

Level 1

Concept: Locate a map scale key.

Objective: Identify the scale key on a map.

Materials: Maps with various scale keys.

Procedure:

1. Show many maps that have a map scale key. Point to the area and draw the scale on the chalkboard.
2. Have several children come up to the maps and point to the map scale keys.
3. Review the importance of scales and when it is necessary to locate the map scale.
4. Discuss the difference in scale on the map. Note the differences not only in appearance, but in the way the numbers are used. For example: some scales have greater numbers than others, some scales use colors and short sequences, some scales use inches, some use feet, others use miles. All maps that are used to determine distance have a map scale. Point out that there is no one standard place for the scale. It can be on the top, bottom, right, or left corners. Children must look for the scale.
5. Ask children what would happen if maps were not drawn to scale.

Enrichment/Extension: Imagine you are in an airplane looking down on a football field. Draw what you would see, including the goal lines, the 50 yard line, and the yard lines in between.

Directions for Worksheet: The worksheet contains map keys. Children will look carefully at all the symbols and circle the three map scales.

From *Helping Your Child with Maps & Globes* published by Good Year Books. Copyright © 1994 by Bruce Frazee and William Guardia.

Where is Scale on a Map?

Directions: Look at the map keys below. Draw a circle around the map scales.

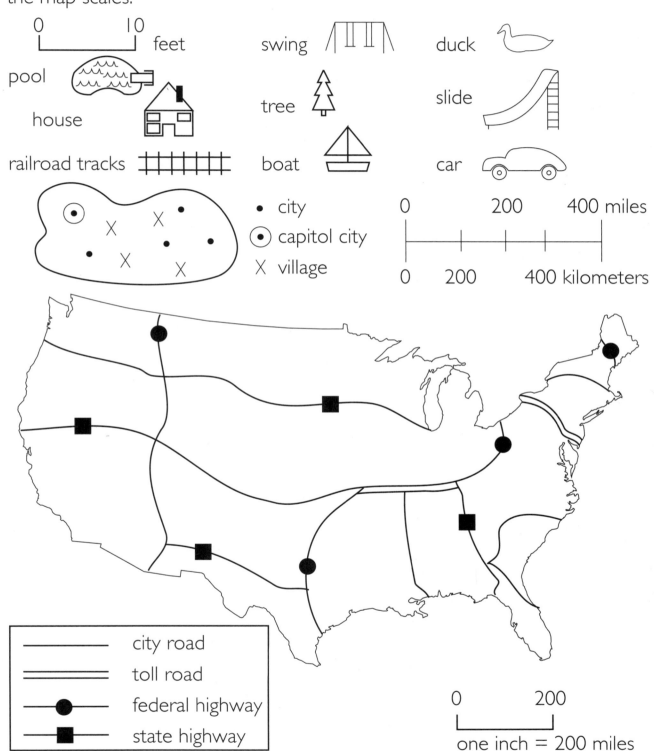

0 _____ 10 feet

pool

house

railroad tracks

swing

tree

boat

• city

⊙ capitol city

X village

duck

slide

car

0   200   400 miles

0   200   400 kilometers

—————— city road

══════ toll road

———●——— federal highway

———■——— state highway

0   200

one inch = 200 miles

How does a Scale Change?

Concept: Understand that scale represents larger, real objects.

Objective: Observe that round objects have a distorted scale when represented on a flat surface.

Materials: Balloons and soft markers.

Procedure:

1. Obtain balloons for each child.
2. Have each child blow up the balloon. Do not tie balloon.
3. Each child then marks a symbol on the inflated balloon with a soft marker.
4. Deflate the balloons.
5. Repeat the same steps except mark a symbol on a deflated balloon and then blow up the balloon.
6. Have children compare the objects drawn according to scale in the inflated and deflated position.

Enrichment/Extension: Look at the continents on the globe. Have children draw the continents on the balloon in the proper locations. Compare and discuss water and land masses.

Directions for Worksheet: Have children draw a picture of their symbol when the balloon is inflated and deflated.

From *Helping Your Child with Maps & Globes* published by Good Year Books. Copyright © 1994 by Bruce Frazee and William Guardia.

Directions: Draw your symbol on the balloon when it was full of air in the large balloon below. Draw your symbol on the balloon when there was no air in it in the small balloon below.

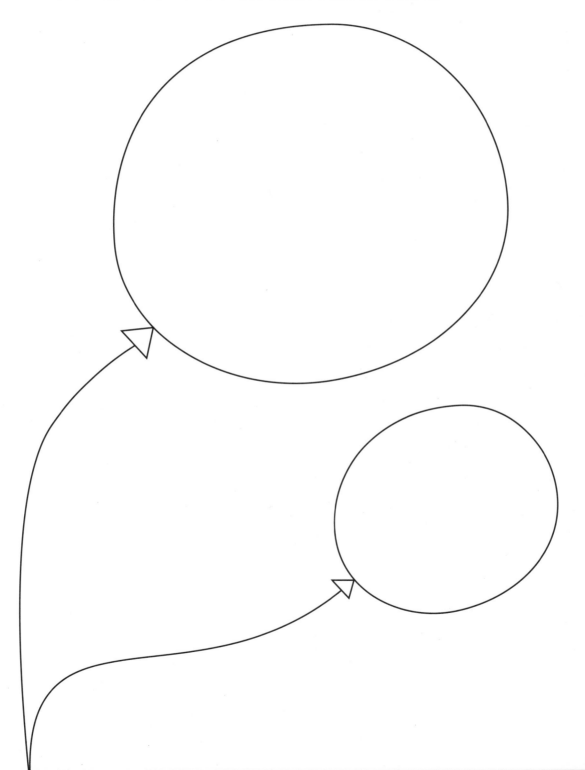

What is a Scale Model?

Level 1

Concept: A model is a representation of a larger object made to fit a smaller scale.

Objective: Show how objects are scaled down to a smaller size.

Materials: Scale car, overhead projector (optional).

Procedure:

1. Explain that a scale model is a smaller version of an object.
2. Obtain a small scale car and place it on its side on the projector. This allows all children to see the car. Move the projector and adjust the focus.
3. Explain that the object they see is still the car but it was made smaller to take up less space.
4. Discuss the need for symbols to be drawn to scale so that more objects could be put on a map.
5. Allow children to put other objects on the projector, such as pencils, keys, shoes, or whatever can fit on top of the projector, to reinforce the concept that larger, real-life objects are still the same, but are shown at a smaller scale.

Enrichment/Extension: Place a number of school objects: stapler, books, pencils, and chalk, on the floor. Have the children stand above and draw the objects to scale on a small sheet of paper. Explain that maps are not only drawn to scale but from a bird's-eye view.

Directions for Worksheet: Hand out a copy of the worksheet to each child. Have them trace their left hand on top of the outlined hand. Discuss the difference in scale and size.

From *Helping Your Child with Maps & Globes* published by Good Year Books. Copyright © 1994 by Bruce Frazee and William Guardia.

What is a Scale Model?

Directions: Put your left hand over the hand below. Trace your hand and color the smaller hand.

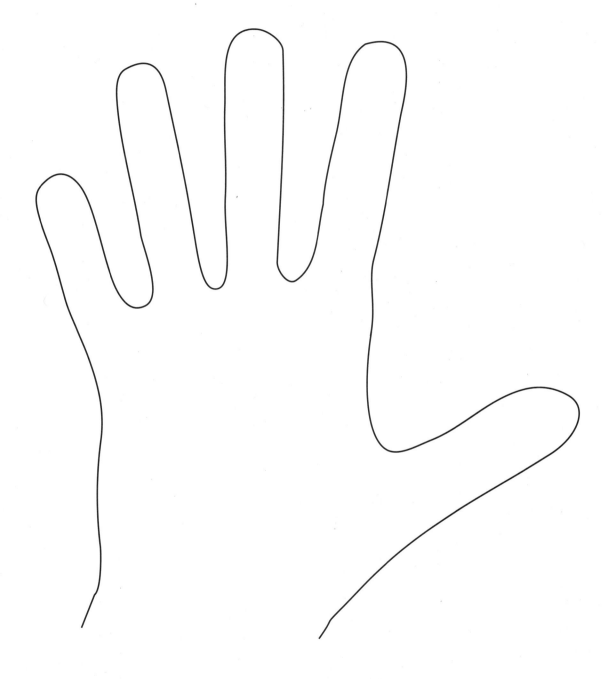

How does Distance Affect Maps?

Concept: Distance reduces size.

Objective: Recognize that the farther they are from an object, the smaller the object appears.

Materials: Chalkboard, overhead projector (optional), and 8" x 11" paper.

Procedure:

1. Draw the picture below on the board.
2. Ask the following questions:
    a. Is cloud #2 as hot or cold as cloud #4 or #5?
    b. If you were on cloud #1 how would your house look? (Small, large, etc.)
    c. How large would your school look from cloud #5?
    d. Will your house look bigger or smaller from cloud #3?

Enrichment/Extension: Place a small object (paper clip, tack) on the floor. View object from close-up and move away from the object. Have children discuss the difference in the views from far and near.

Directions for Worksheet: Have children draw a picture of an animal in each of the kites. Ask children how these pictures differ? How are they alike?

From *Helping Your Child with Maps & Globes* published by Good Year Books. Copyright © 1994 by Bruce Frazee and William Guardia.

How does Distance Affect Maps?

Directions: Draw a picture of an animal in each of the kites. Color in your animals.

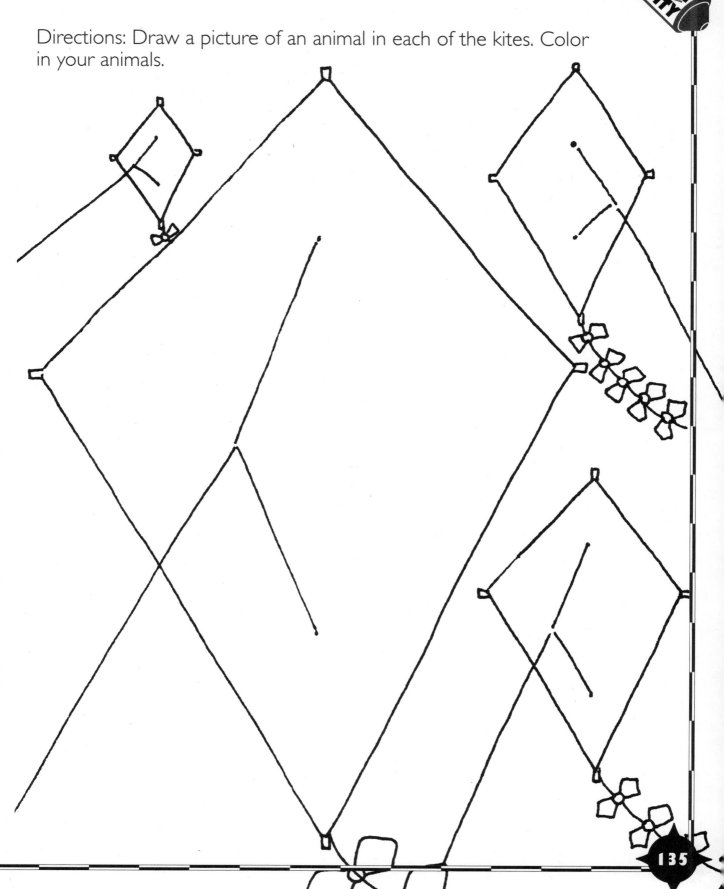

From *Helping Your Child with Maps & Globes* published by Good Year Books. Copyright © 1994 by Bruce Frazee and William Guardia.

How do You Make a Scale Map?

Level 2

Concept: A map is a two-dimensional representation of the three-dimensional environment.

Objective: Create a two-dimensional scale map of a community.

Materials: A large sheet of butcher paper, match boxes, crayons, and glue.

Procedure:

1. Draw an outline map of various streets, rivers, airports, etc, like the example below, on a piece of butcher paper 5' × 6'.

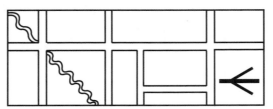 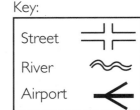

Key:
Street
River
Airport

2. Assign children to groups to build match box houses, churches, schools, and businesses to place on the spaces in the community map.
3. Add other important symbols of a community. For example: fire hydrants, trees, other necessary buildings, and/or physical features.
4. Discuss the buildings and symbols in terms of scale. Objects need to be proportionate to the real-life objects. Discuss big/small, near/far, long/short, and cardinal directions.

Enrichment/Extension: Make a grid and put it over the community. Have children play location games to find various buildings, streets, and symbols by their location on the grid. Have children use rulers to check proportion of scale in their community to ensure that objects are of approximate size. Children can also measure distance between objects with rulers.

Directions for Worksheet: Give each child a copy of the worksheet. Have them stand over the community and draw a smaller scale of their community in the space on the worksheet. Allow children to approximate scale; assist them in developing a map scale and key.

From *Helping Your Child with Maps & Globes* published by Good Year Books. Copyright © 1994 by Bruce Frazee and William Guardia.

How do You Make a Scale Map?

Directions: In the space below, draw a smaller scale picture of your community. Stand over the community and look down on it for a bird's eye view and draw what you see.

Scale   **Key**

Level 2

Concept: Use an object of a certain length to determine scale and distance.

Objective: Devise a scale and measure distance between objects in the classroom.

Materials: String, rulers, and several state or local maps.

Procedure:

1. Have children determine the length of their desk or table in hands.
2. Have children use various objects to compute the length, width, or height of the room.
3. Pass out a 4" piece of string to each of the children. Let them compute the number of units of string that are needed for the width of their desk or table top, the length, width, or height of the room, etc.
4. Show how the 4" pieces of string were used as a scale to measure the distance between places. Explain that scale is a common unit and then the unit is converted into actual distance. For example: 4 inches × 12 pieces of string = 48 inches or 4 feet.
5. Discuss the value of a scale; how impossible it would be to have the actual distances drawn on maps instead of scale distances.

Enrichment/Extension: Using state or local maps, use the scale of miles to compute actual miles between several known landmarks or cities.

Directions for Worksheet: Have children use a ruler to determine the distance between places on the worksheet.

From *Helping Your Child with Maps & Globes* published by Good Year Books. Copyright © 1994 by Bruce Frazee and William Guardia.

How do You Measure Scale?

Directions: Use a ruler to answer the questions below.

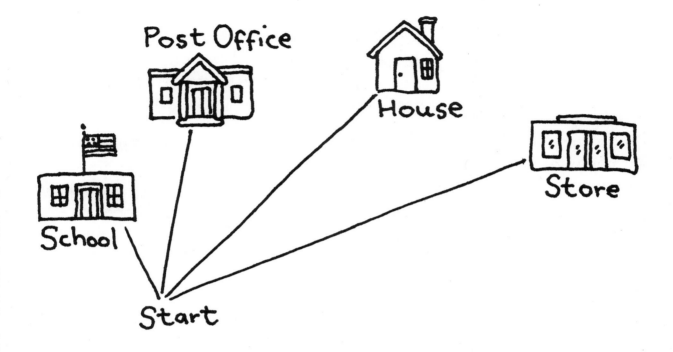

1. Put the ruler on START. Measure and count the number of inches from START and write in the space below:

From START to the POST OFFICE: _____ inches.

From START to the STORE: _____ inches.

From START to the HOUSE: _____ inches.

From START to the SCHOOL: _____ inches.

2. If an inch is equal to a yard, how many yards is it from START to the HOUSE? _____ yards.

If an inch is equal to a mile, how many miles is it from START to the HOUSE? _____ miles.

What is the Distance Between my Classroom and the Playground?

Concept: Map scale can change but the distance remains the same.

Objective: Compare various map scales over a constant distance.

Materials: Masking tape, ball of string, and several maps with different size scales.

Procedure:

1. Explain that the scale of miles might be different on various maps, but the distance is the same.
2. Compare several maps with different scales. Point out that maps with a larger scale are smaller with regard to the picture, or community they see. Maps with a smaller scale are larger. Both show the same actual distance.
3. Put children into groups of five. Cut four lengths of string, 30 feet, 20 feet, 10 feet, and 5 feet for each group. Mark a spot in the classroom START. Measure a distance of 300 feet to the playground and mark END.
4. Give children the worksheet and explain the directions.
5. Review the procedure of adding groups. For example: if you have 5 lengths of string, you used 5 sets or groups. If the length of the string is 10 feet, you have a distance of 50 feet.

   10 + 10 + 10 + 10 + 10 = 50 feet

Enrichment/Extension: Substitute the metric system of measurement. Children do the same worksheet with meters instead of feet. Convert to show distance is still the same no matter which string (scale) is used.

Directions for Worksheet: Show children the START line in the classroom and the END line on the playground. Each group will receive a 30, 20, 10 and 5 feet length of string. Children will measure the distance between these two points with each length of string for a different scale. Children must count the number of lengths used to compute the distance for each length of string. Review the example on the worksheet. Have groups begin the activity.

From *Helping Your Child with Maps & Globes* published by Good Year Books. Copyright © 1994 by Bruce Frazee and William Guardia.

Distance to Playground

Directions: Measure the distance from START to END as explained by your teacher. Use each length of string and count the number of lengths used from the start to the finish. Mark the number of times each piece of string was used in the space below for each length of string. When you finish measuring add the number of times you used each length to determine the distance.

For example: A piece of string is 10 feet long. Between START and END you used the string 5 times to measure the distance. Since the string is 10 feet and you have 5 groups of 10, you add: 10 + 10 + 10 + 10 + 10 = 50 feet.

Show the number of times you used each length of string and the distance from START to END for each length in the chart below.

Lenth of String	Number of Times	Distance
1. 30 feet	_____	_____
2. 20 feet	_____	_____
3. 10 feet	_____	_____
4. 5 feet	_____	_____

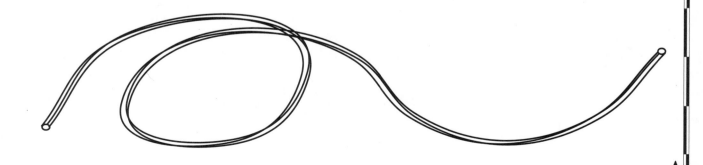

From *Helping Your Child with Maps & Globes* published by Good Year Books. Copyright © 1994 by Bruce Frazee and William Guardia.

How is Distance Found on a Map?

From *Helping Your Child with Maps & Globes* published by Good Year Books. Copyright © 1994 by Bruce Frazee and William Guardia.

Level 2

Concept: Covert scale on a map to actual distance.

Objective: Compute distances between cities using a map's scale of miles legend.

Materials: Various maps with scales, and rulers.

Procedure:

1. Using a wall map, a globe, and a textbook map, have children locate the scale for measuring distance.
2. Allow children to compare and contrast the different scales.
3. Show children how to place a ruler on the scale strip and mark the conversion. Then have them add the number of units to equal the total number of miles between places.
4. Assign cities for children to locate and then, using the scale of the various maps, compute the actual miles between the cities.

Enrichment/Extension: Locate various types of maps, all of the same general area or state. Break children into groups and have children compare the legends. List cities or landmarks common to all maps. Have each group compute actual miles between cities. Compare each group's answer with the other groups.

Directions for Worksheet: Have children measure the scale strips with their rulers. Note that one inch equals 100 miles and two inches equals 200 miles. Stress that the scale is one inch for every 100 miles. Have children measure and convert the distance between the places on the worksheet.

How is Distance Found on a Map?

Directions: Measure the distance between the cities asked in each question. Convert every inch into 100 miles. Put the total number of miles for each question.

● Carson

● Beaver

● News

⊙ Capitol

● Jam

Key: ● City
⊙ Capitol

Scale: 1 inch = 100 Miles

| 1" | | 1" |
0   100   200

1. How many miles is it from the Capitol to Carson? _____ miles

2. How many miles is it from Jam to Carson? _____ miles

3. How far is it from Beaver to News? _____ miles

4. How far is it from the Capitol to News? _____ miles

5. How far is it from Beaver to Carson? _____ miles

Level 2

Concept: Changing scale to compute distance.

Objective: Measure distances between various cities using scale and conversion.

Materials: Rulers.

Procedure:

1. Explain that you need to use a scale key to determine the distance between object on a map.
2. Give each child a copy of the worksheet and a ruler.
3. Using the worksheet and the rulers, lead children through the following steps.
   a. Find Bugs and Spuds on the map.
   b. Place one end of the ruler on Bugs and the other end on the paper so its edge touches Spuds.
   c. Count the inches between where it begins at Bugs and where it passes through Spuds.
   d. Use the scale to figure out how many miles between Bugs and Spuds.
4. Allow children to work independently, in groups, or teacher-directed to convert the scale of miles for these cities.
   a. Bugs to Myrtle.
   b. Bugs to Nimbell.
   c. Spuds to Flussome.
   d. Spuds to Blickmore.
   e. Other cities on worksheet for practice.

Enrichment/Extension: Use the atlas and other maps so children can practice using different scales to convert distance.

Directions for Worksheet: Have children locate cities and learn how to properly place their rulers between cities and determine distance using the scale. Some children may need help in approximating scale to miles when fractions of a distance are involved.

From *Helping Your Child with Maps & Globes* published by Good Year Books. Copyright © 1994 by Bruce Frazee and William Guardia.

How do you Convert Scale?

Directions: Listen carefully to your teacher and follow the directions using a ruler to measure distance.

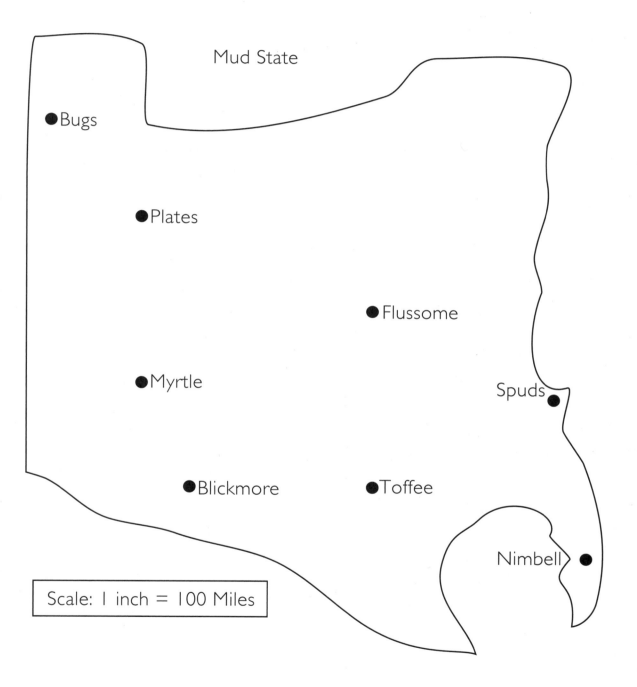

Mud State

● Bugs

● Plates

● Flussome

● Myrtle

Spuds ●

● Blickmore   ● Toffee

Nimbell ●

Scale: 1 inch = 100 Miles

From *Helping Your Child with Maps & Globes* published by Good Year Books. Copyright © 1994 by Bruce Frazee and William Guardia.

Why are Maps Drawn to Different Scales?

Concept: Maps are drawn to different scales to save space and show details.

Objective: Compare maps to different scales to interpret various details and distances.

Materials: Globe, state map, and local map.

Procedure:

1. Show the globe and point to your state. Show a state map and then a local map. Compare the likenesses and differences between the maps. Show that the distances are the same even though the scale changes. Reinforce the fact that map distance is smaller, but the real distance when converted is the same.

2. Discuss scale as showing real distance in a smaller form. Distances on maps must be made smaller than the real distances on earth. Therefore, a certain number of inches is equal to a certain number of feet or miles, depending on the scale.

3. Hand out the worksheet and ask these questions as children observe the three maps and their scales.

   a. Which map is most useful to see Washington, D.C. in relationship to other states?

   b. Which map is most useful to see the states around Washington, D.C.?

   c. Which map shows the neighborhood of Washington, D.C.?

   d. Which map has the largest scale?

   e. Which map has the smallest scale?

Enrichment/Extension: Have children use the rulers and map scales to determine the distance between two points.

Directions for Worksheet: Use directed teaching and lesson questions to help children make comparisons between map scales and distances.

From *Helping Your Child with Maps & Globes* published by Good Year Books. Copyright © 1994 by Bruce Frazee and William Guardia.

Maps Drawn to Different Scales

Directions: Look at the three maps. Look at the details and the scales to answer questions.

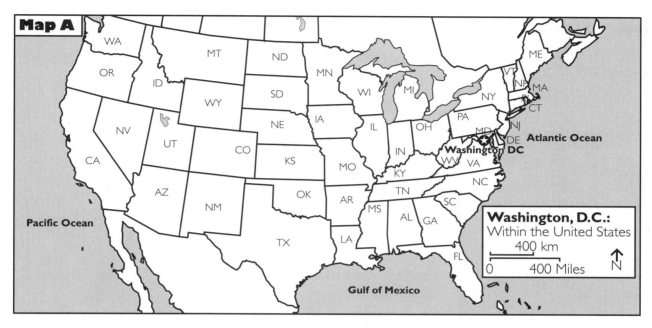

Map A

WA, OR, ID, MT, ND, MN, WI, MI, ME, VT, NH, MA, NY, RI, CT, PA, NJ, WY, SD, IA, IL, IN, OH, MD, DE, NV, UT, CO, NE, KS, MO, WV, VA, **Washington DC**, CA, AZ, NM, OK, AR, KY, TN, NC, SC, MS, AL, GA, TX, LA, FL

Atlantic Ocean

Pacific Ocean

Gulf of Mexico

Washington, D.C.: Within the United States
400 km
0   400 Miles

Map B

West Virginia

Maryland

• Frederick

Baltimore

Leesburg

Washington D.C.

Annapolis

Alexandria

• Culpepper

Cambridge

Fredericksburg •

Virginia

Chesapeake Bay

Richmond •

Farmville •

Petersburg •

Washington D.C.: Neighboring States
100 km
100 Miles

Map C

Silver Spring

University of Maryland

190

Connecticut Ave.

Wisconsin Ave.

16th Ave.

Rock Creek Park

WASHINGTON

Anacostia River

American University

National Zoo

Howard University

National Arboretum

Memorial Pkwy

Georgetown University

New York Ave.

White House

Union Station

Constitution Ave.

U.S. Capitol

Arlington National Cemetery

Independence Ave.

The Pentagon

295

Washington National Airport

395

5

Alexandria

Potomac River

95

Washington, D.C.: Downtown
0   5 Miles
0   5 Km

How Does a Scale Work on a Grid?

Level 1

Concept: Understand scale on a grid system.

Objective: Take small parts of a map (the area in one grid) and expand it to be complete in itself.

Materials: 9" × 12" paper, 12" × 18" paper, scotch or masking tape, and crayons or markers.

Procedure:

1. Copy the map from the worksheet. Cut it into grid sections equal to the number of children in the class. For example: 25 children = 25 grid squares or a grid system that is 5 grids across and 5 grids down. Include a symbol in each grid.
2. Number the grids on the back. Assign each child one grid to enlarge on a 9 × 12 in. paper.
3. After children enlarge their own square, the entire class assembles a larger map made up of the smaller grid pieces.
4. Compare the scale of the newly created map with that of the worksheet map.

Enrichment/Extension: Obtain two maps of various sizes, each representing the same location. For example: compare a local detailed city road map with a small road atlas map of the same city. Compare a large wall map of the United States with a smaller textbook map.

Directions for Worksheet: Make a copy of the worksheet for each child. Make one copy and cut into squares equal to the number of children in the class. Give each child a larger sheet of paper 9" × 12" to draw a larger picture of their square.

From *Helping Your Child with Maps & Globes* published by Good Year Books. Copyright © 1994 by Bruce Frazee and William Guardia.

How Does a Scale Work on a Grid?

Directions: Look at your individual section of the map. Draw a larger picture of your section on another sheet of paper.

How are Latitude and Longitude Used to Find Distance?

Concept: Latitude lines measure distance north and south. Longitude lines measure east and west.

Objective: Understand the more lines of latitude and longitude you cross the greater the distance.

Materials: Paper, crayons, overhead projector (optional), and transparency.

Procedure:

1. Copy the worksheet on an overhead transparency.
2. Show examples of city or other maps with latitude and longitude on grids.
3. Put the transparency on the projector and ask questions, such as: If you start from 10° latitude and travel north on Longitude 120° to Latitude 50°, how many latitude blocks did you pass? (Answer: 4) What are the numbers of the intersection where you stopped? State that the approximate distance between one degree of latitude and longitude at the equator is 70 miles and 0 miles at the poles. Show latitude and longitude on the globe.

Enrichment/Extension: Let children draw a city and make a grid using latitude and longitude. Have children locate various places on their maps using their grid system. Have children determine which places are near and far according to the number of lines of latitude and longitude that were passed.

Directions for Worksheet: Copy the worksheet on a transparency. Distribute copies of the worksheet for children to mark as you locate and pass various lines of latitude and longitude. Compute with children various locations marked on the worksheet.

From *Helping Your Child with Maps & Globes* published by Good Year Books. Copyright © 1994 by Bruce Frazee and William Guardia.

Latitude and Longitude

Directions: Find the places marked below with your teacher and answer the questions below.

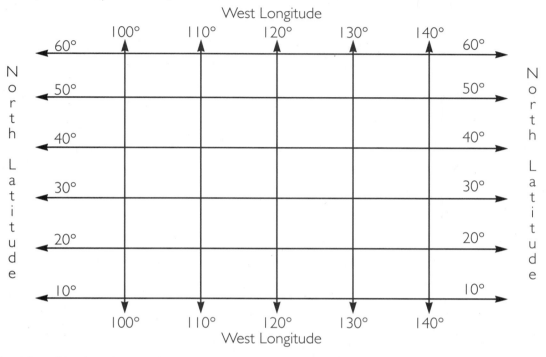

1. 1° of latitude and longitude is equal to _____ miles.

2. Start at 50° N latitude and 100° W longitude and move to 50° N latitude and 120° W longitude. How many miles of longitude did you travel? 20 x 70 miles = _____

3. Start at 10° N latitude and 110° W longitude. Move to 60° N latitude and 110° W longitude. How many miles of latitude did you travel? 50 x 70 miles = _____

4. Make two more moves of latitude and longitude with your teacher. Write the latitude and longitude and the miles traveled in the space below:

   ___°N lat ___°W long TO ___°N lat ___°W long = ___ miles

   ___°N lat ___°W long TO ___°N lat ___°W long = ___ miles

5. Do one latitude and longitude by yourself.

From *Helping Your Child with Maps & Globes* published by Good Year Books. Copyright © 1994 by Bruce Frazee and William Guardia.

How can you Compute Distance and Time?

Concept: Interpret direction by using the sun.

Objective: Find north by facing your shadow and note that shadows are different sizes at different times.

Materials: Rulers and worksheet.

Procedure:

1. Take the children to the playground or backyard at 9:00 a.m.
2. Locate the cardinal directions.
3. Have children draw a straight line on the ground from east to west.
4. Children will be placed on the line and their shadows will be measured.
5. Repeat the 9 a.m. activity at 10 a.m., 11 a.m., 12 p.m., 1 p.m., and 2 p.m.
6. Children will chart the differences in the shadows and note that the shadows are always north of the east-west line.
7. Children will form generalizations, using their information. Examples: "The sun helps us locate cardinal directions." "Shadows are shortest around noontime."

Enrichment/Extension: Construct a sundial using a shoebox top with a pencil glued to the center of the box top. Take the sundial outside and orient it to north. At various hours during the day, mark the box with the specific time where the shadow of the pencil hits. The next day, check the accuracy of the box with the classroom clock.

Directions for Worksheet: Give children a copy of the worksheet and ask them to keep a record of their shadows at various times during the day.

From *Helping Your Child with Maps & Globes* published by Good Year Books. Copyright © 1994 by Bruce Frazee and William Guardia.

Computing Distance and Time

Directions: Measure your shadow at different times during the day.

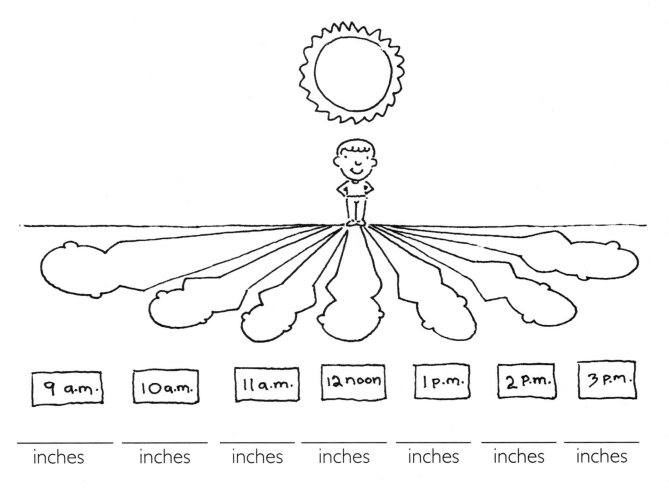

| 9 a.m. | 10 a.m. | 11 a.m. | 12 noon | 1 p.m. | 2 p.m. | 3 p.m. |

| inches | inches | inches | inches | inches | inches | inches |

1. When is your shadow the longest? _____

2. When is it the shortest? _____

3. What other objects cast shadows? _____

_____

_____

_____

Chapter Five: The Globe

Teaching Children About The Globe

As children begin to understand and work with maps, they should also begin to locate places on the globe. Initial study begins with examining globes to discover the size and shape of the globe when compared to a flat map. Familiar locations can be discussed and located on a map and then compared to the same area on the globe. The areas of land, water, and other earth features can also be located on the globe and compared to features on a map. The teacher and parent should use every opportunity possible to compare and refer to the globe when studying maps because the globe shows the whole earth. Early exposure to the globe is essential because it shows worldwide relationships. A globe is necessary to show and demonstrate important concepts taught in these lessons.

The following activities will provide children with readiness skills before they begin the lessons that follow for this chapter:

1. Compare and classify various surfaces outside such as: hard, soft, smooth, rough, grass, sand, etc. Show photographs and magazine pictures to children to view and categorize various earth surfaces.

2. Develop a chart to classify things on land or water. Discuss how land, water, and air make up most of the earth.

3. Draw pictures of events that take place on land, water, and in the air. For example, volcanos, high waves in the water, and clouds in the air.

4. Observe the sun, moon, and stars during different times of day. Point out positions and shapes of each.

5. Inflate a balloon without tying the end. Have children draw a picture on the balloon. Release the air and discuss how the balloon's picture changed as the air was released. Let children see the distortion of the picture while you discuss how hard it is to show round earth (globe) in a flat way (flat map). Stress and show with a globe that the earth is round. Show children a wall map and a globe to compare.

6. Observe clouds, rain, and other weather features. Talk about the weather everyday with words like sunny, cold, warm, cloudy, and so forth.

From *Helping Your Child with Maps & Globes* published by Good Year Books. Copyright © 1994 by Bruce Frazee and William Guardia.

7. Discuss how the earth moves (around the sun). Show how the earth moves by having children hold a ball or balloon. Ask children to rotate the balloon, with their arms extended and keeping the balloon in a centered position, while they are also moving in a circle around the balloon.

8. Make papier-mache out of strips of paper and paste made from flour and water. Wrap the strips around objects to make various objects such as: a balloon could show the earth, egg cartons to make hills, boxes for mountains, and so forth.

9. Identify land masses in different parts of the globe, starting with the North American continent. Discuss land masses (continents) and water (oceans).

10. Make a bulletin board with green longitude lines and red latitude lines, using a different color to identify the equator, Tropic of Cancer, and Tropic of Capricorn.

11. Discuss shapes such as: round, circle, half-circle, sphere, hemisphere. Cut an apple in half crosswise and show children the northern and southern hemispheres of the apple. Then cut an apple in half lengthwise to demonstrate the western and eastern hemispheres. Children can then choose part of a hemisphere to eat.

Skills to be Acquired: The Globe

1. Recognizes that the earth is basically round.

2. Understands that the globe is a model (representation) of the earth.

3. Identifies oceans (water) and continents (land) and discovers there is more water than land.

4. Compares maps to the globe.

5. Uses a globe to identify areas discussed.

6. Locates his/her own state, country, and continent on a globe.

7. Locates north and south on a globe.

8. Understands the globe is divided into hemispheres.

9. Locates the equator, tropics, and poles on a globe.

10. Recognizes color as symbols on a globe.

From *Helping Your Child with Maps & Globes* published by Good Year Books. Copyright © 1994 by Bruce Frazee and William Guardia.

11. Locates topographical features and places on a globe.

12. Identifies imaginary north-south east-west lines on a globe.

13. Understands why we have day and night.

14. Learns the days of the week and can properly order them.

15. Learns the months of the year.

16. Understands yesterday, today, and tomorrow.

17. Identifies directions of sunrise and sunset.

18. Identifies the relationship of the sun to the time of day.

19. Understands the earth's motion around the sun (relation and revolution).

20. Understands that the globe is the only true representation of the earth (map distortion).

21. Understands the relationship between sea level, elevation, and altitude.

Where is Land and Water?

Concept: Discriminate between land and water on a globe.

Objective: Construct a globe to learn that the earth contains land masses and water masses.

Materials: Styrofoam balls/balloons, brown construction paper, pins or glue, and a classroom globe.

Procedure:

1. Obtain styrofoam balls or balloons.
2. Have children draw out seven circles on brown construction paper. Each circle is to represent the land masses (continents).
3. Have children attach the land masses 1 through 7 to a balloon or styrofoam ball.
4. Discuss the fact that the earth has 7 major land masses (continents) and the rest of the earth is water.
5. Compare children's globes to the classroom globe.

Enrichment/Extension: Use papier mache to make globes and have children paint the mache blue for water and brown for land. Compare the mount of land mass to water mass pointing out that there is more water on earth than land.

Directions for Worksheet: Explain that the worksheet shows one half of the earth. Tell the children to color the land green and the water blue.

From *Helping Your Child with Maps & Globes* published by Good Year Books. Copyright © 1994 by Bruce Frazee and William Guardia.

Where is Land and Water?

Directions: Color the land green and the water blue. Put the right colors in the map key.

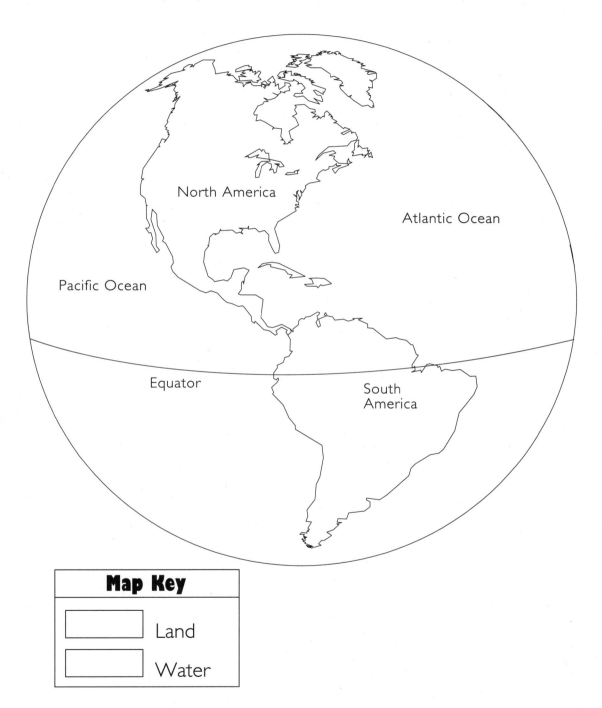

Map Key

	Land
	Water

Where are the Continents and Oceans?

Concept: Continents on the globe.

Objective: Recognize water (ocean) and land (continents).

Materials: 8" x 11" paper, construction paper, potato chip canisters, globe, wall map of world, copies of a world map.

Procedure:

1. Have each child bring a cylindrical potato chip canister to class.
2. Give children a copy of the worksheet showing the seven continents drawn symbolically as circles or oblongs.
2. Make children aware that each shape represents a continent.
3. Prior to covering the canister, children may color the continents and the waters of the ocean.
4. Compare a wall map with the sheet of paper before the canister is covered with the map.
5. Have children cover a potato chip canister with the paper of circles and oblongs.
6. Point out the various continents on the commercial globe and point to the circle on the canister that represents the respective continent. Also point out the five oceans of the world.
    Antarctic Ocean   Arctic Ocean
    Atlantic Ocean   Indian Ocean
    Pacific Ocean
7. Save canisters for the following equator activity.

Enrichment/Extension: Give children a copy of a real world map. Have them superimpose the map on their "globe" canister and identify the continents and oceans on their new globe.

Directions for Worksheet: Give children a copy of the worksheet and have them color the continents and waters of the ocean. Then have them place the map on the canister to make a globe. Discuss the differences and similarities between the canister "globe" and a real globe.

From *Helping Your Child with Maps & Globes* published by Good Year Books. Copyright © 1994 by Bruce Frazee and William Guardia.

Finding the Continents and Oceans

Directions: Color the continents and oceans. Place the colored map over the canister to make a "globe."

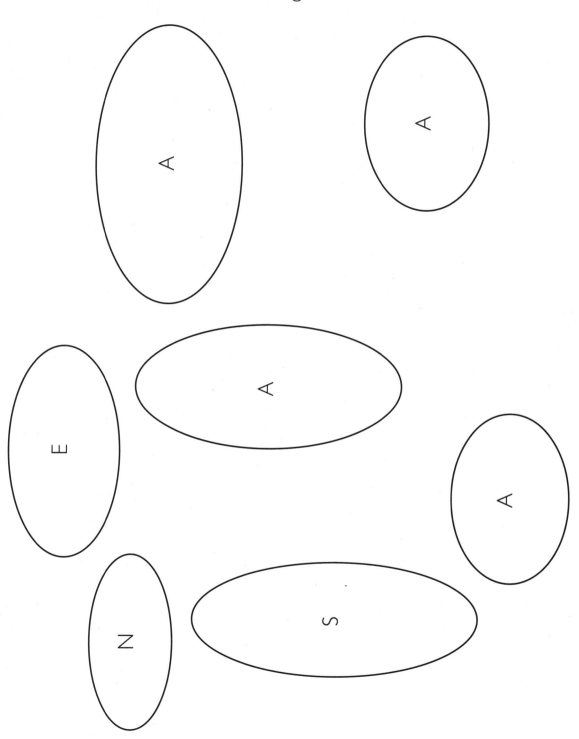

From *Helping Your Child with Maps & Globes* published by Good Year Books. Copyright © 1994 by Bruce Frazee and William Guardia.

Where is the Equator?

Concept: Special degrees of latitude.

Objective: Locate major points north and south of the equator.

Materials: Cylinder-shaped potato chip canister from previous "Globe" activity.

Procedure:

1. Direct children's attention to the Equator, North Pole, and South Pole on the worksheet.
2. Cover the canisters with the worksheet.
3. Explain that the canister represents the planet earth. Ask children what is different about this globe as compared to a real globe.
4. Locate, on the "globe" and a world map, the equator and the poles.
5. Direct children to hold the globe in the middle, by the Equator. Then, ask children to hold the globe by the North Pole and South Pole.
6. Locate the tropics on the globe and world map. North of the equator is the Tropic of Cancer. South of the equator is the Tropic of Capricorn.
7. Use the canister to help with children's school supplies.

Enrichment/Extension: Continue to identify other locations and latitudes as the children progress in learning the concept of degrees north and south of the equator.

Directions for Worksheet: Have children locate the equator and poles on their copy of the worksheet before following the procedure for the lesson.

From *Helping Your Child with Maps & Globes* published by Good Year Books. Copyright © 1994 by Bruce Frazee and William Guardia.

Where is the Equator?

North Pole

Tropic of Cancer

Equator

Tropic of Capricorn

South Pole

What are Hemispheres?

Concept: Identify northern, southern, eastern, and western hemispheres.

Objective: Understand the difference between the four hemispheres.

Materials:
Construction paper, glue, scissors, gummed stars, string, hole puncher, pins.

Procedure:

1. Cut two construction paper circles three or four inches in diameter. Mark the four cardinal directions on the circles. Then cut four half-circles of the same radius, but of a contrasting color to the whole circles. Glue two half-circles to each circle, one to each side, positioned so that one circle represents north and south hemispheres and the other circle represents east and west hemispheres.

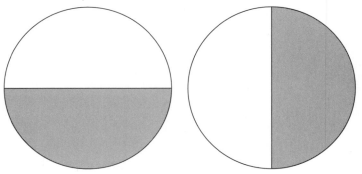

2. Explain that the northern and southern, and eastern and western hemispheres are half of the globe, like the half-circles are halves of the whole circles.

3. Have each child construct their own hemispheric world design using the worksheet.

Enrichment/Extension:

1. A string can be attached through a hole punched in the top of the circle and world designs can be hung from the ceiling.

2. Contrasting colors appropriate to different seasons (i.e.: orange and black for October, red and green for December) may be used.

3. A small gold or silver gummed star may be placed in the appropriate hemisphere to indicate the child's home.

Directions for Worksheet:

Have children cut the circle out and place their construction paper half-circles on it to make their own world design.

From *Helping Your Child with Maps & Globes* published by Good Year Books. Copyright © 1994 by Bruce Frazee and William Guardia.

What are Hemispheres?

Directions: Cut out the circle below and place your construction paper half-circles on it to make a world design with hemispheres.

How does the Earth Move?

Concept: Rotation of the earth.

Objective: Understand that the planet earth rotates every twenty-four hours on its axis as it goes around the sun.

Materials: Globe and canisters.

Procedure:

1. Help children sing the song "Around and Around It Goes."
2. Ask children to make circles with their arms and hands as they sing the song.
3. Demonstrate the concept by taking a globe and rotating it on its axis and at the same time taking the globe around its orbit; the teacher representing the sun.
4. Give each child a canister to represent the earth and have them rotate it and take it on its orbit.

Enrichment/Extension: Children may follow this lesson by learning what causes the "four seasons" of the year.

Directions for Worksheet: Hand out copies of the song. Have one child rotate a globe around a sun while children sing the song.

From *Helping Your Child with Maps & Globes* published by Good Year Books. Copyright © 1994 by Bruce Frazee and William Guardia.

Around and Around it Goes

A-round and a-round and a-round it goes as it goes a-round the sun. This pla-net earth is the home of man-kind. A-round and a-round and a-round it goes as it goes a-round the sun. Three hun-dred and six-ty five days it takes to go a-round the sun. A-round and a-round and a-round it goes as it goes a-round the sun. Yip-pe-i-ay, yip-pe-i-o, yip-pe-i-ay, yip-pe-i-o!

Around and around and around it goes as it goes around the sun.
This planet earth is the home of mankind.
Around and around and around it goes as it goes around the sun.
Three hundred and sixty-five days it takes to go around the sun.
Around and around and around it goes as it goes around the sun.
Yippie i-a, Yippie i-o, Yippie i-a, Yippie i-o.

From *Helping Your Child with Maps & Globes* published by Good Year Books. Copyright © 1994 by Bruce Frazee and William Guardia.

Why do we have Day and Night?

Level 1

Concept: Rotation of the earth causes day and night.

Objective: Identify the reason for day and night.

Materials: Desk lamp/flashlight and globe.

Procedure:

1. Select 24 children, each one to represent one hour in a day.
2. Have children form a circle, then face outward and hold hands.
3. Have children move counterclockwise to demonstrate the rotation of the earth at the equator.
4. The teacher or a parent can represent the sun as children rotate.
5. Periodically stop the rotation to ask children if they see the sun (teacher/child). The person directly in front of the sun represents noon, the person directly across from noon represents midnight. The children to the sun's left are morning and to the sun's right, afternoon. If the child cannot see the sun without turning his or her head, it is nighttime.

Enrichment/Extension: Obtain a classroom globe. Mark your state and city on the globe. Station a desk lamp or flashlight so its rays hit the globe. As every minute passes move the globe counterclockwise to demonstrate the relationship rotation to day and night.

Directions for Worksheet: Have children look at the events on the worksheet and circle the things they do during the day.

From *Helping Your Child with Maps & Globes* published by Good Year Books. Copyright © 1994 by Bruce Frazee and William Guardia.

Why do we have Day and Night?

Directions: Circle the activities you do during the day.

When are Yesterday, Today, and Tomorrow?

Level 1

Concept:
Understanding the days of the week.

Objective: Recognize daily cycles as a repetitive pattern.

Materials: Paper and index cards.

Procedure:

1. Place a piece of paper on the floor with the word Wednesday on it.
2. Ask children: If today is Wednesday, what was yesterday? (Move one step to the right.) If yesterday was Tuesday and today is Wednesday, (return to Wednesday block) surely tomorrow will be Thursday. (Move one step to the left of Wednesday's block.
3. After children have recognized that Tuesday is followed by Wednesday, etc. mention all the days of the week, each time taking a side step to the right asking: Where are we?

Enrichment/Extension: Put the days of the week on index cards. Shuffle cards and let children put the cards in order.

Directions for Worksheet: Have children fill in the events of yesterday on the worksheet. List the events of today up to the corresponding hour. Have children predict what they will do for the remainder of the day and tomorrow.

From *Helping Your Child with Maps & Globes* published by Good Year Books. Copyright © 1994 by Bruce Frazee and William Guardia.

Yesterday, Today, and Tomorrow

Directions: Write a word to describe what you did for each hour under Yesterday, Today, and what you predict you will do for the rest of Today and Tomorrow.

Night	Afternoon	Morning	
			24 hours

Tomorrow

Night	Afternoon	Morning	
			24 hours

Today

Night	Afternoon	Morning	
			24 hours

Yesterday

From *Helping Your Child with Maps & Globes* published by Good Year Books. Copyright © 1994 by Bruce Frazee and William Guardia.

What will I do Next Week?

Level 1

Concept: Days of the week.

Objective: Know the days of the week and place them in order.

Materials: Copies of poem and large paper with names of the days of the week.

Directions for Worksheet: Give children a copy of the worksheet and have them fill in the blank days. Have children keep worksheets for two weeks and each day spend some time discussing activities for that day and have them draw a symbol on that day's square. Another idea is to give children a new word each day; give the definition. Write various sentences and make sure children know how to spell the new word. At the end of the two weeks have a spelling contest.

Procedure:

1. Have children memorize the poem: "One Long Week."

One Long Week

What am I going to do next week?
    Probably on Sunday,
    I will go to the park.
And I know that on Monday,
    I will go to school.
On Tuesday, I will go to the library and
    I will check out a book.
I know that Wednesday
    is the middle of the week.
The next day is Thursday
    and I will visit my grandmother.
And on Friday,
    I can stay up late
Because on Saturday,
    I have one extra hour in bed.
And again I ask myself:
What am I going to do next week?
    On Sunday? On Monday? On Tuesday?
    On Wednesday? On Thursday, Friday
    and Saturday?

2. Name seven children as days of the week.
3. Mix children's order, and then ask children to stand in the correct order. For example: Sunday through Saturday.
4. Name the days of the week sequentially and an event that has taken place.

Enrichment/Extension: List all things you would like to do next week for each day.

From *Helping Your Child with Maps & Globes* published by Good Year Books. Copyright © 1994 by Bruce Frazee and William Guardia.

What will I do Next Week?

Directions: Fill in the top boxes with the correct day of the week. Fill in the bottom boxes with an event or word your teacher assigns for each day.

Saturday				Friday	
Friday				Thursday	
Wednesday					
				Tuesday	
Monday				Monday	
Sunday					

From *Helping Your Child with Maps & Globes* published by Good Year Books. Copyright © 1994 by Bruce Frazee and William Guardia.

What are the Seasons?

Concept: Earth and sun's relationship to the seasons of the year.

Objective: Compare and develop concepts of summer, fall, winter, and spring.

Materials: Paper 36" x 5", crayons/markers, pencils, and rulers.

Procedure:

1. Children will have a strip of paper 36 inches long (36" x 5").
2. Children will fold the strip of paper into four sections.
3. Children will unfold the strips of paper and select a color for each section and color each section identifying each section as spring, summer, fall, and winter.
4. Children will further divide each section in three, writing the names of the months for each season.

Spring			Summer			Fall			Winter		
March	April	May	June	July	August	Sept.	Oct.	Nov.	Dec.	January	February

Enrichment/Extension: Children may continue and identify a holiday for each season.

For Example: Spring = Passover/Easter
Summer = 4th of July
Fall = Halloween
Winter = Christmas/Hanukkah

Directions for Worksheet: Read the poem on the worksheet to children. Have them write their own season poem.

From *Helping Your Child with Maps & Globes* published by Good Year Books. Copyright © 1994 by Bruce Frazee and William Guardia.

What are the Seasons?

Directions: Read the poem, then write your own poem about your favorite season below.

Season Poem
Color me green, I am Spring. Color me red, I am Fall.
I am Winter, Feel me cold. I am Summer, Feel me warm.
And when it rains, Feel me wet.
In the Winter, I feel cold. In the Summer, I feel warm.
And when it rains, I feel wet!

My Season Poem

_____

_____

_____

_____

_____

_____

_____

_____

_____

Where is the Sun?

Concept: Rotation of the earth around the sun.

Objective: Determine the hour of day by the shadow of an object at various times during the day.

Materials: Copies of the poem and rulers.

Procedure:

1. Read the following poem to children:

    The Moving Earth
    The sun shines
        in the morning
        at noon
        and in the afternoon.
    The sun continues to cast
        shadows
        'til sunset.
    spotlighting
        certain things
    and casting shadows
        on other things.

2. Draw a line from east to west out in the ground.
3. Place a child at a certain point.
4. Measure the shadow of the child starting at 9 a.m. and continue until 2 p.m. hourly.
5. Log all hourly measurements and illustrate.

Enrichment/Extension: Have children illustrate "The Moving Earth."

Directions for Worksheet: Have children use the worksheet to log in shadow measurements of an object and illustrate.

From *Helping Your Child with Maps & Globes* published by Good Year Books. Copyright © 1994 by Bruce Frazee and William Guardia.

Where is the Sun?

Directions: Pick an object for shadow measurement. Write down the measurements of its shadow beginning at 9 a.m. and continue until 2 p.m. Illustrate the length of the shadows below.

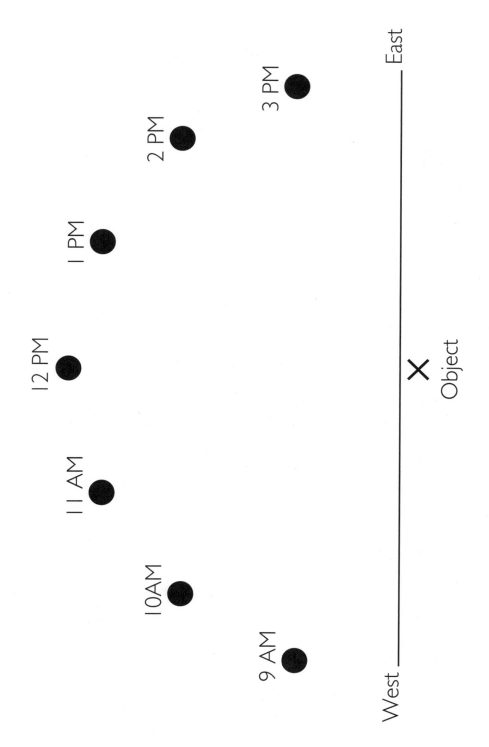

From *Helping Your Child with Maps & Globes* published by Good Year Books. Copyright © 1994 by Bruce Frazee and William Guardia.

Level 2

Concept: 24 hours make a day.

Objective: Understand the earth rotates every twenty-four hours.

Materials: Paper, pencils, and construction paper.

Procedure:

1. Give each child a copy of the worksheet and ask them to cut out the two strips.
2. Have children assign the first twelve sections to be the a.m. and the next twelve sections to be the p.m. Number each section one through twelve. Draw the two halves on the board and number to illustrate for the children while they are making their own.
3. Read children the poem "The Day Begins."

    The Day Begins

    The day begins when
        the school bell rings
    And the day is already
        eight hours old
    But my day begins
        when the alarm clock rings.
    The day is twelve hours old
        at high noon.
    The day begins at midnight.
    When does your day begin?

4. Explore the hour strip while reading the poem. Ask children to determine what time it is according to the poem. For example, for "And the day is already eight hours old," children should be able to determine it is eight o'clock in the a.m.

Enrichment/Extension: Place the hour strip around the globe with 12 o'clock noon placed over your state. After placing the strip of paper on a globe, ask children to determine when the day begins in different parts of the world. For example: While it is 12 o'clock noon in your state, what time is it in another country, or in another part of the U.S.?

Directions for Worksheet: Give each child a copy and have them write 1–12 on each half and color the a.m. section of the day yellow and the p.m. section blue.

From *Helping Your Child with Maps & Globes* published by Good Year Books. Copyright © 1994 by Bruce Frazee and William Guardia.

Where does the Day Begin?

Directions: Cut out each strip. Assign a number 1 through 12 for each section on the strips. Color one strip yellow for the daytime, a.m., and color the other strip blue for the nightime, p.m.

Do Day and Night have a Pattern?

Concept: Days and nights have recurring cycles.

Objective: Recognize the day and night cycles as a repetitive pattern.

Materials: 9" × 12" paper, black coloring markers, crayons.

Procedure:

1. Ask children to fold a white piece of 9" × 12" paper in half, in half again, and once more. Have them open the paper. It should have 8 sections.
2. Instruct children to use a dark color to create a checkered pattern effect, coloring in every other square. The second square should be the first dark square.
3. Label light squares "day" and the dark squares "night."
4. Discuss that day follows night and night follows day. Relate this phenomenon to the words "pattern" and "repetition."
5. Position a globe in front of the children. Using a sticker or other marker to locate your state, rotate the globe. As the children see the marker, have them say "day." As the marker revolves out of sight, they say "night." Point out that their words will form a pattern as you continue to rotate the globe.

Enrichment/Extension: Day and night patterns can be drawn on black paper using white crayon or chalk to create the "days." Children can also explore the globe to determine when it is day and night for other countries of the world.

Directions for Worksheet: The worksheet has a copy of the 8 sections the children's paper should have. Ask them to color every other section and mark each box Day or Night. As you proceed with 5. of the lesson, stop at several different countries to determine whether they are in daytime or nighttime and have children write the names of those countries on the worksheet according to their day or night pattern.

From *Helping Your Child with Maps & Globes* published by Good Year Books. Copyright © 1994 by Bruce Frazee and William Guardia.

Directions: Color every other section and write Day on the white sections and Night on the black sections. Write the names of countries from around the world in each section according to whether they are in daytime or nighttime.

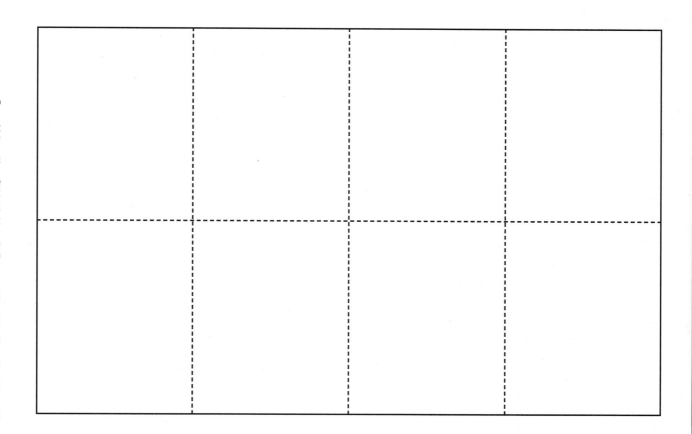

What Makes a Month?

Level 2

Concept: Days make a month.

Objective: Classify days with dates.

Materials: Paper 31" x 4" and crayons or markers.

Procedure:

1. Begin a discussion on the days of the week where you ask: If the 1st day of the month is Friday, what will the 2nd day be? Continue questioning through and including the 8th day.
2. Children may want to know how many hours are in one day, one week, one month, and how many hours of daylight are in a particular month in their area.
3. Ask children the following questions: Do you want to go to sleep earlier during the week as compared to the weekend? How many hours do you spend in school? How many hours do you spend watching television? How many hours do you spend doing your homework?

Enrichment/Extension: Beginning the lesson on the 1st day of the month would allow for the following activity: Have one or two children make a large "Ribbon in Space" calendar, an appropriate length to fit over the chalk or bulletin board. As each day of the month progresses, a child may cross off one day.

Directions for Worksheet: Have children take a particular month and place the day over the date. For example: If the 1st is on Wednesday, the 2nd will be Thursday. Identify important dates during that month.

From *Helping Your Child with Maps & Globes* published by Good Year Books. Copyright © 1994 by Bruce Frazee and William Guardia.

What Makes a Month?

Directions: Fill in the correct numbers on the calendar.

Sunday	Monday	Tuesday	Wed.	Thurs.	Friday	Saturday
		1				

Where are the Tropics?

Concept: Location of the equator, tropics and poles.

Objective: Identify the equator, tropics, and poles.

Materials: overhead projector (optional), transparency, potato chip canister, glue, and crayons or markers.

Procedure:

1. Point out the equator, poles, and tropics on the globe.
2. Make a cylinder from file folders or paper 8 1/2" x 11".
3. Make a transparency from the worksheet. Place it on the projector and discuss the equator, poles, and tropics. Let children draw and label on a sheet of paper the equator, poles, and tropics.
4. Discuss and color various continents and oceans.

Enrichment/Extension: Cut an orange in half. Remove contents keeping the skin of both halves intact. Try to flatten the skin. Discuss distortion and the problem of representing the round earth on a flat surface.

Directions for Worksheet: Make a transparency of the worksheet. Have children come up to the projector and color various areas located on the transparency. Check these areas on the globe.

From *Helping Your Child with Maps & Globes* published by Good Year Books. Copyright © 1994 by Bruce Frazee and William Guardia.

Where are the Tropics?

North Pole

Tropic of Cancer

Equator

Tropic of Capricorn

South Pole

What are the Time Zones?

Concept: Time zones in the United States.

Objective: Determine the time in cities which are in various time zones in the United States.

Materials: Worksheet.

Procedure:

1. Give children a copy of the worksheet. Discuss the fact the United States map is divided into four sections or time zones.

2. Discuss the different time zones using specific examples, such as: If it is two o'clock in Chicago, Illinois, it is noon in Albequerque, New Mexico.

3. Explain to children the reasons for time zones. Because the earth rotates, the sun's position moves around the world. Therefore, if it is two o'clock in Chicago, the earth has rotated further past the sun than in Albequerque, where it is noon.

Enrichment/Extension: Reinforce the rotation of the earth, that is, it is daylight in New York City before it is daylight in Dallas, Texas. Use other examples to help illustrate this point.

Directions for Worksheet: Assign a time for one time zone clock. Ask children to determine the other three times in each time zone. Also locate different cities in the United States, asking children to plot these cities on their map and determining what time it is according to the time zones.

From *Helping Your Child with Maps & Globes* published by Good Year Books. Copyright © 1994 by Bruce Frazee and William Guardia.

Directions: After your teacher assigns one clock, find the times in the other time zones. Plot different cities on the map and determine what time it is in that city according to its time zone.

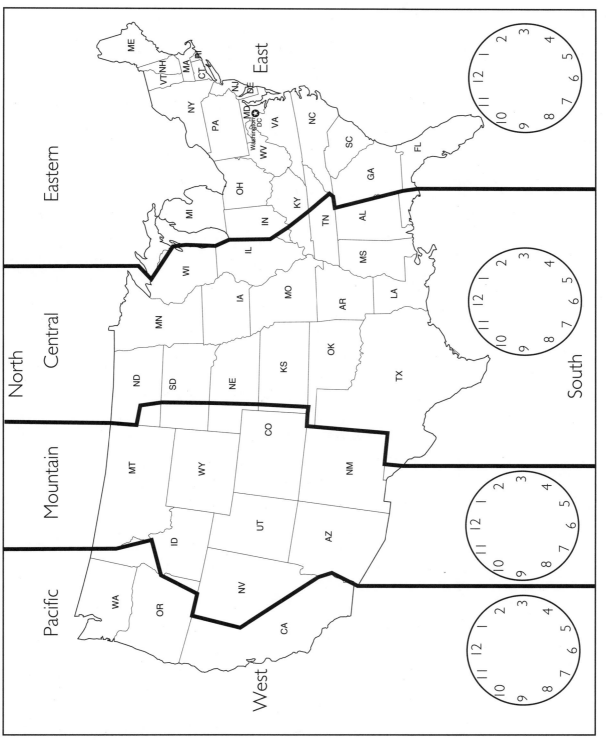

From *Helping Your Child with Maps & Globes* published by Good Year Books. Copyright © 1994 by Bruce Frazee and William Guardia.

What Makes a Year?

Level 2

Concept: The year is divided by seasons and months, weeks, and days.

Objective: Recognize that a year is divided into 365 days, twelve months and four seasons

Materials: 9 1/2" × 4" envelopes, index cards, crayons.

Procedure:

1. Have children learn the following poem:
   One More Year

   One, two, three,
       three months old.
   Four, five, six,
       six months old.
   Seven, eight, nine,
       nine months old.

   Ten, eleven, twelve,
       twelve months old.
   One more year.
   Happy Birthday
       one more time.
   Happy Birthday
       again and again.

2. Hand out one envelope and one index card and a copy of the worksheet. Ask children to illustrate their envelope and divide their index card according to the worksheet.

3. Ask children to cut one short end of the envelope to make a slit. Insert the index card. As the children recite the poem, they pull out part of the index card that corresponds to the line they are reciting. For example, in "One, two, three, three months old," the children pull out the first line of months, 1-2-3.

4. Discuss with children that each three months represents a season and after twelve months a year has passed.

Enrichment/Extension: People's growth can also be explored through the envelope's illustration of a person's head and shoulders. As each year is drawn out, that person grew bigger, smarter, healthier, etc. Children from different grade levels or ages may be brought to class to compare their heights at different ages. If possible, photograph groups of children with different heights.

Directions for Worksheet: Give each child a copy of the worksheet to help them illustrate their envelopes and divide their index cards.

From *Helping Your Child with Maps & Globes* published by Good Year Books. Copyright © 1994 by Bruce Frazee and William Guardia.

Directions: Use the example below to help you divide your index card into months and seasons.

| 10 | 11 | 12 |

| 7 | 8 | 9 |

| 4 | 5 | 6 |

| 1 | 2 | 3 |

Where will I go in the World?

Concept: Mobility of people.

Objective: Understand that products and ideas come from all over the world because people move from their homelands.

Materials: World maps and encyclopedias.

Procedure:

1. Divide the children in groups of five.
2. Assign each group a country they will visit. Each group will select five items they will take as gifts to that country. Each group should also select an ideal value of American society to introduce to that country. Have children show their route and method of transportation on a world map.
3. Ask each group to report to the class the route and method of transportation they used in getting to their country and information they learned.

Enrichment/Extension: "Visitors" from the various visited countries will present to the class. Each group can be asked to bring a suitcase back from their country containing five gifts from that country. For example, you may suggest children bring back music or art work that represents the country's culture. Children can find books or music for their country in the library or resource center.

Directions for Worksheet: Discuss their gifts and the gifts they bring back from their visiting country. Children can complete the worksheet with their gifts and new information.

From *Helping Your Child with Maps & Globes* published by Good Year Books. Copyright © 1994 by Bruce Frazee and William Guardia.

Where will I go in the World?

Directions: Show on the map the route your group took to get to the country you visited. Complete the questions below.

A. Gifts from the United States

1.

2.

3.

4.

5.

Gifts from the country you visited:

1.

2.

3.

4.

5.

B. Draw a picture of the flag from the country you visited.

C. Write any new information learned about the country you visited to present to the class.

_____

_____

_____

_____

_____

Where are Latitude and Longitude on a Globe?

Concept: Latitude and longitude lines on a globe.

Objective: Identify latitude and longitude on a globe.

Materials: Papier mache globe, and copies of the poem.

Procedure:

1. Read children the poem:

   ### Different Degrees

Latitude, going north	Standing there
Latitude, going south	Where the west begins
Getting there	Standing there
From here to there	Where the east ends
By the numbers, by degrees	Standing there
Is quite a task.	Where the south begins
Longitude, going east	Standing there
Longitude, going west	Where the north ends
Getting there	Standing there
From here to there	Where peace begins
Is quite a task.	Standing there
	With a smile.

2. Discuss with children, using a globe, how lines of latitude become shorter as they progress from the equator to the North or South Poles. Longitude lines become narrow as they approach the North or South Poles.

3. Using a papier mache globe, draw the parallel lines of latitude red and longitude lines green. Reinforce the Equator and Tropics lines of latitude.

Enrichment/Extension: Assign an independent study on the Horse Latitudes (regions where trade winds blow toward the equator). Discuss the earth's rotation causing the winds of the Northern Hemisphere to turn to their right, thus the trade winds blow from the northeast rather than the north. The trade winds of the Southern Hemisphere turn to their left, becoming southeast winds. Have children illustrate the routes of the trade winds.

Directions for Worksheet: Use the worksheet to visualize the latitude lines for 2. of the lesson.

From *Helping Your Child with Maps & Globes* published by Good Year Books. Copyright © 1994 by Bruce Frazee and William Guardia.

Latitude and Longitude on a Globe

Directions: Use the illustration below to help you understand how latitude lines become shorter as they approach the North Pole.

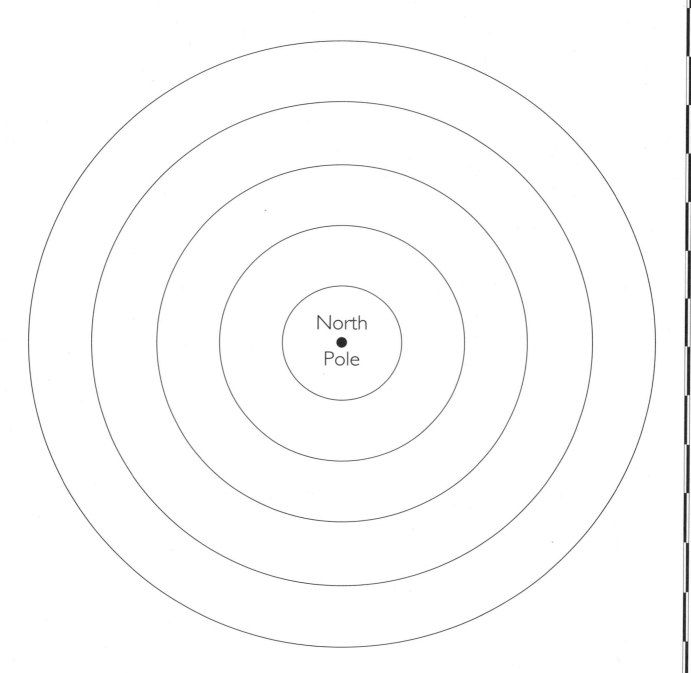

North
Pole

From *Helping Your Child with Maps & Globes* published by Good Year Books. Copyright © 1994 by Bruce Frazee and William Guardia.

Why is a Globe Accurate?

Concept: Differences between global maps (round) and wall maps (flat).

Objective: Understand the accuracy of a globe is highest because it is the closest representation of the earth.

Materials: Balloons, papier mache materials, crayons and different types of world maps.

Procedure:

1. Ask children to construct a globe using papier mache on a balloon.
2. When the globe is ready, have children illustrate the continents and oceans. Then cut the globe in half and flatten each half.
3. Compare a globe's representation of continents and a wall map's representation. Children should notice that in a flat map, continents maintain their true shapes, but their relative sizes, compared to a globe, are distorted.
4. Discuss the earth's shape, emphasizing that it is round. The most accurate way of representing the earth is with a sphere.

Enrichment/Extension: Obtain four different types of world maps: A Robinson projection, a Mercator projection, an Azimuthal projection, and a Molleweide projection. Explore each one with children and discuss each map's distortion compared to a globe.

Directions for Worksheet: Discuss with children the differences between a global map and a flat map as illustrated on the worksheet.

From *Helping Your Child with Maps & Globes* published by Good Year Books. Copyright © 1994 by Bruce Frazee and William Guardia.

Why is a Globe Accurate?

Directions: Look at both maps and compare.

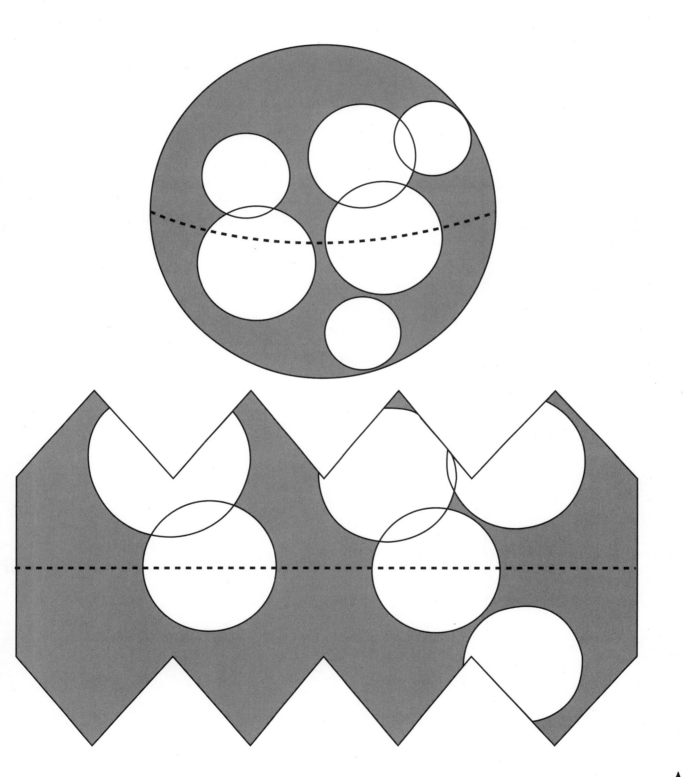

Appendix A

Additional Resources

The following is a list of resources that can help parents and teachers acquire materials and information for their children.

Local government offices, especially those dealing with public transportation, often provide free road maps.

State tourist agencies and local chambers of commerce publish walking tour maps or guidebooks to area attractions.

The Federal Government has hundreds of maps available. For a comprehensive listing, contact the Government Printing Office (GPO) bookstore in your area or the Superintendent of Documents, Government Printing Office, Washington, DC 20402. The GPO handles the printing and sales of items produced by government agencies.

Maps from the U.S. Geological Survey, the civilian mapmaking agency of the United States Government, covering a range of areas including National Wildlife Refuges to LANDSAT pictures of the Earth. For a catalog, write to the Earth Science Information Center, U.S. Geological Survey, 507 National Center, Reston, VA 22092.

A wide selection of material is available from the National Aeronautics and Space Administration (NASA), 400 Maryland Avenue SW, Washington, DC 20546. For a full list, ask for a copy of *NASA Educational Publications.*

Helping Your Child Learn Geography, published in cooperation with the Department of the Interior, U.S. Geological Survey. Send your name, address, and 50 cents to: Geography, Consumer Information Center, Pueblo, CO 81009.

Exploring Your World: The Adventure of Geography. This National Geographic book contains an easy-to-use index, cross references, and a wall map of the world. For orders, inquiries, and catalogs, write to National Geographic Society, Educational Services, Washington, DC 20036. Or call 1-800-368-2728.

Geography Education is organized around five fundamental themes. Copies are available for $20 ($15 for orders of three or more) from Phi Delta Kappa, P.O. Box 789, Bloomington, IN 47402-0789. Or call (812) 399-1156.

Weekly Reader provides Skills Books, particularly "Learning Basic Skills with U.S. Geography" (grades 4–6) and "Learning Basic Skills with Geography" (grades 2–3). For a Weekly Reader catalog of products or to order, call 800-999-7100.

Appendix B

Glossary of Geographic Terms

Azimuthal Projection: A map using a projection that shows true compass direction.

Business: The buying and selling of things; trade.

Cardinal Directions: Any one of the four main directions on the compass; north, south, east, and west. They may be shown on a map. For example, north is not always at the top of a map.

City: A large area where many people live and work.

Community: A group of people who live together in the same place.

Compass: An instrument for showing directions, consisting of a needle or compass card that points to the north magnetic pole, which is near the North Pole.

Compass Rose: A graduated circle, usually marked in degrees, indicating directions.

Continent: Large bodies of land. The continents are Africa, Antarctica, Asia, Australia, Europe, North America, and South America.

Country: An area of land that has boundaries and has a government that is shared by all the people; nation.

Days of the Week: The 24 hours of one day and night. We have seven days in a week: Sunday, Monday, Tuesday, Wednesday, Thursday, Friday, and Saturday.

Direction: Can be determined by the poles on a map. Terms such as north, south, east, west, southeast, etc., can be used to describe directions.

Distance: The amount of space between two things or points.

Earth: A huge sphere comprising of land and water masses.

Elevation of Land: Measured from sea level.

Equator: An imaginary circle around the Earth halfway between the North Pole and the South Pole; the largest circumference of the Earth.

Globe: A small, round model of the earth. It is the most accurate representation of the earth.

From *Helping Your Child with Maps & Globes* published by Good Year Books. Copyright © 1994 by Bruce Frazee and William Guardia.

Grid System: An arrangement of vertical and horizontal lines to locate a specific place on the earth, globe, or map.

Hemisphere: Half of the earth, either vertically or horizontally. If sectioned vertically, they are western and eastern hemispheres. If sectioned horizontally, they are northern and southern hemispheres.

Horse Latitudes: The areas 30° north and south of the equator characterized by trade winds that blow toward the equator.

Immediate Environment: The exact place and area where you are located such as a bedroom or classroom.

Intermediate Directions: Halfway between the cardinal directions: northwest, northeast, southwest, southeast.

Land: The part of the earth's surface that is not under water.

Latitude: Distance measured on the earth's surface north and south of the equator. On a globe or map, lines of latitude are drawn running east and west. Latitude is expressed in degrees. Each degree is equal to approximately sixty miles.

Location: The place where something is located; site.

Longitude: Distance measured on the earth's surface east and west of an imaginary line. On a globe or map, lines of longitude are drawn from the North Pole to the South Pole. Longitude is expressed in degrees.

Map: A drawing that shows all or part of the earth. Maps of large areas usually show cities, rivers, oceans, and other features.

Map Key (Legend): A listing which contains symbols, meaning of colors, and other information about a map.

Map Projections: Provide different perspectives on the sizes and shapes of areas shown. Global projections, or globes, are more accurate than flat maps because flat maps represent a round object on a flat surface. This causes distortion of sizes and shapes.

Map Scale: The size of a plan, map, or model compared with what it represents. The scale of the map is one inch for every 200 miles.

Mercator Projection: A global map; land masses retain their true shapes, but the projection distorts the relative size of land masses.

Mile: A measure of distance equal to 5280 feet.

Molleweide Projection: A global map; an equal-area projection that shows relative size accurately, but distorts shapes.

Month: One of the twelve parts of a year.

Neighborhood: A small area of district in a town or city where people live.

Oceans: The entire body of salt water that covers nearly three- quarters of the earth's surface; any one of the five separate oceans: the Atlantic, Antarctic, Arctic, Indian, or Pacific.

Pictograph: A graph that uses pictures to show information.

Poles: Either end of the earth's axis. The North Pole is opposite the South Pole.

Polar Regions: The Arctic and Antarctic Circles are imaginary lines that define the polar regions.

Positional Terms: Words that show the position or location of an object, such as above, below, on, off, under, around, etc.

Prime Meridian: Zero degrees longitude; passes through Greenwich, a suburb of London.

Products: Anything that is made or created.

Reference System: Use of information to describe the location of one object to another. The self is a reference system as well as landmarks, grids, and so forth.

Relative Location: Can be expressed in terms of left, right, near, far, above, below, up, and down.

Robinson Projection: A global map; a compromise projection because it maintains no single property, like true shape, size, or compass direction, but minimizes overall distortion.

Rotation of the Earth: Results in day and night; rotates through 15 degrees of longitude every hour.

From *Helping Your Child with Maps & Globes* published by Good Year Books. Copyright © 1994 by Bruce Frazee and William Guardia.

Scale: On a map or globe; makes it possible to determine distances between places.

Season: One of the four parts of the year; spring, summer, fall, or winter.

State: A group of people living in a political unit that is part of a larger government.

Symbols: Something that stands for or represents real things.

Trade Winds: Winds blowing steadily toward the equator from about 30° north latitude or 30° south latitude.

Time Zones: The earth is divided into 24 hour time zones.

Tropics: The Tropic of Cancer and Tropic of Capricorn are lines of latitude lying north and south of the equator. The region of the earth between them is known as the Tropics.

Water: The liquid that is found over the earth in the form of oceans, lakes, rivers, and ponds.